SHAKESPEARE
(*from a sketch by T. L. Poulton*)

SHAKESPEARE

by JOHN DRINKWATER

Great Lives

LONDON
GERALD DUCKWORTH & CO. LTD.
NEW YORK
THE MACMILLAN COMPANY

First published January 1933
Reprinted 1933, 1949 *and* 1957

First published in the United States in 1956

Printed by Offset litho
in Great Britain by
Phototype Ltd., London

CONTENTS

To
ARCHIBALD FLOWER
*who has done so much
to provide for* Shakespeare
*a living memorial in his
native town*

NOTE

IT is difficult at this time of day to write about Shakespeare without being anywhere controversial. In a book which may be read by many people who have made no special study of Shakespeare, it seemed necessary, for example, to say something on the question of disputed authorship. Everyone knows that it has been raised, and silence might be mistaken for evasion. I have used Mr. Percy Allen's book as my text for a little plain speaking on the matter because he is the ablest advocate of what I take to be the most up-to-date heresy. I hope I have done so without acrimony. At any rate, I am sure that we should enjoy the plays together.

Still less would I have any fractious note creep into my differences with so fine a scholar and so helpful a critic as Mr. Dover Wilson. In my opposition to some of his views, I hope that he will feel at least that I have conducted myself as becomes a Gentleman's Disagreement.

Controversy, however, is but incidental to a book in which I have attempted to report as simply as I could what Shakespeare has meant to a working man-of-letters, in and out of the theatre. For this purpose I have kept my mind steadily on the plays in the living environment of the stage for which they were created. The little we know of Shakespeare's life is, marginally, a valuable aid to our understanding of his work, and I have told it without embellishment. On only one obscurity have I indulged in speculation. That so much about Shakespeare should be unknown, I do not find disturbing, but the problem of his retirement in 1611 insists on some explanation. I claim no more for mine than that it is plausible to myself, while no other is.

J. D.

Highgate,
September 1932

CHAPTER I

PROLOGUE

THIS brief study of Shakespeare makes no profession of scholarship by the highly specialised standards that have been applied to the subject. It is not even informed by any exhaustive knowledge of all that such scholarship has achieved. Mr. Dover Wilson's textual restorations ; Mr. Leslie Hotson's conquests in the Record Office ; Mr. Percy Allen's indefatigable search for windmills at which to go a'tilting in honour of his Dulcinea, Oxford ; the major charting of the whole spacious times by Sir E. K. Chambers and Mr. Percy Simpson – I can admire such exploits with gratitude, but I cannot emulate them.

The experts themselves would allow with me that there is a great deal about Shakespeare the poet and Shakespeare the man that awaits elucidation ; a great deal, probably, that will never be elucidated. But for myself, I may as well go beyond this and confess at once that these obscurities cause me no disquiet. I am, I suppose, but an indifferent seeker after truth. The fact is that there are many passages in Shakespeare's plays that I do not understand, many problems of his dramatic career on which I have no opinion, and many popular conundrums about his life to which

I can offer no answer. But it is the fact also **that** I do not mind. I have even been shameless enough, when I was producing Shakespeare's plays in the theatre, to let the audience make what it could of the difficulties without over-taxing my own wits to explain them.

No one will ever disentangle finally the spurious passages from the authentic Shakespeare ; the exact dates, even the exact order of the plays will in some cases remain doubtful ; we shall never reach uniform agreement as to the sense of a hundred confusions, and of many of them we shall never make any sense at all. Similarly, the rewards of research, exciting as they often are, can hardly hope to expand our knowledge of the poet's life in any fundamental respect. Mr. Hotson's *Shakespeare versus Shallow*, for example, is a brilliant piece of investigation based on the shrewd discovery of a single clue. We cannot grudge the author his satisfaction ; indeed, we share it as we follow his patient exposition. Such work is eminently worth while, and a credit to scholarship. But it should be regarded in proper perspective. In a volume of substantial length, Mr. Hotson establishes two facts : that Justice William Gardiner and not Sir Thomas Lucy was the original of Mr. Justice Shallow, and that *The Merry Wives of Windsor* belongs to the year 1597, whereas hitherto it has usually been assigned to 1598 at earliest. Admirable, but not necessitating any revision of our views about Shakespeare.

The industry and often the understanding that characterise Shakespearean scholarship deserve nothing but our respect. In the accumulation of three hundred years they have helped in many ways to facilitate our approach to Shakespeare himself. No encouragement that they can be given in the future will be misplaced. But one fact of capital importance has to be noted. If we possessed nothing but the printed editions of the plays (1623), *Venus and Adonis* (1593), *Lucrece* (1594), and the *Sonnets* (1609), together with such a collection of contemporary or traditional evidence as that supplied by Mr. Pierce Butler in his *Materials for the Life of Shakespeare* (1930), we should substantially know as much as we now do, and, it must be added, as much as is necessary for a sound view of Shakespeare's genius and its spiritual occasion. If we amplify these with some knowledge of the political and social conditions that he knew, we can further visualise the environment of his genius without much difficulty.

No one to-day would be so foolish in his enjoyment of Shakespeare as to neglect the assistance that later scholarship can give him. The work that has been lavished on the text, for instance, while it has sometimes been indiscreet, on the whole relieves our minds of many perplexities. But we must not forget, in our gratitude to a long succession of editors, that the supreme editorial achievement remains the great folio that was undertaken and seen through the press by John

Bs

Heminge and Henry Condell with Edward Blount, the publisher, in 1623, seven years after Shakespeare's death.

Moreover, the care given to the elucidation of difficulties has tended to create an impression that Shakespeare is altogether a difficult subject. A poet who has inspired so much erudition must, it might seem, be accessible only to the erudite. In such a mood we are apt to overlook the fact that ninety-nine per cent of Shakespeare is plain as a pike-staff to the ordinary person of no erudition at all, and that most scholastic enterprise is engaged on the one per cent which isn't.

This book, then, makes no contribution to Shakespearean scholarship, nor will it be much concerned with the problems to which that scholarship is chiefly directed. It is written for those people who, liking Shakespeare, may derive some satisfaction from hearing one who shares their liking discuss his reasons for it. I have made but little special preparation for the occasion. Of the vast literature known as Shakespeareana I can claim no intensive knowledge, and I have now no inclination to repair the defect. I have from time to time read a few of the more important works on the subject, and consulted others as necessity arose ; but I should be ploughed in any recondite test.

On the other hand, English poetry for thirty years has been a constant habit of my mind, which means that the works of Shakespeare have supplied a considerable part of my life's experience. My reading of the plays has been guided by no plan, and some of them I know far more familiarly than others. But their substance as a whole I know as well as I am ever likely to know anything by book-learning, and to their significance I have applied an understanding that they themselves have largely helped to form. My preferences are often difficult to defend in logic, but they are decided, even obstinate. Nothing, for example, can persuade me that Falstaff of *The Merry Wives* is the lifeless caricature of himself that most critics seem to find him. I think, on the contrary, that his creator took him to the domestic scene at Windsor without any loss of comic mastery. Nor, as I shall explain later, do I believe that any good purpose can be served by refusing to recognise that even at the height of his powers Shakespeare could sometimes, like lesser men, make serious errors of constructive judgement.

In addition to frequent reading of the plays for no other reason than that they gave me pleasure, and availing myself of as many opportunities as possible of seeing them performed, I have produced and acted in several of them myself – a dozen at a guess – at Barry Jackson's Repertory Theatre at Birmingham, thereby coming at close grips with them on the stage for which they were intended. For our productions in those days, though not actually employing the Elizabethan model, preserved, with their double platform and apron, the constructional principle that Shakespeare used, without which, I am still convinced, no performance of his plays can be wholly satisfactory.

If this book pretends to add nothing to Shakespearean scholarship, neither does it share the belief which has lately been manifesting itself that Shakespeare somehow stands in need of rehabilitation. Mr. Dover Wilson is the ablest exponent of this curious idea. Nothing is more unseemly in a critic than the scolding of others who have worked over his ground, and if I devote a few lines to scolding Mr. Wilson, it is only to scold him for scolding. I admire his very engaging book, *The Essential Shakespeare*, in everything but his exposition of the reason that caused him to write it, which, he says, is that he " heartily dislikes some of the current interpretations which pass as orthodox, and has long wished to work out another which might seem more in accord with common sense and with what we know of the life and spirit of other poets and creative artists." He then proceeds to rate Sir Sidney Lee, and to attribute to his *Life* the chief responsibility for a false image of Shakespeare that it seems has taken possession of the popular mind. He supports this view by quoting Lee's remark, " His [Shakespeare's] literary attainments and successes were chiefly valued as serving the prosaic end of making a permanent provision for himself and his daughters," adding that " the image in Lee's heart was that of a typical English manufacturer who happened to deal in *Twelfth Nights* and *Lears*, instead of brass tacks." This image, we go on to learn, was drawn by Lee partly from Halliwell-Phillips, and partly from " frequent visits to Stratford," where he allowed his judgement to be impaired by the memorial bust in the church, which, Mr. Wilson says, " might suit well enough with an affluent and retired butcher, but does gross wrong to the dead poet." Then, in conclusion, " The Stratford bust, and Lee's *Life*, inspired by gazing too much upon it are together, I am convinced, mainly responsible for the campaign against ' the man of Stratford ' and the attempts to dethrone him in favour of . . . whatever coroneted pretender may be in vogue at the present moment."

Here is a strange misconception. The attempts to dethrone Shakespeare derive from very different causes. Nor is there any evidence of which I know that this idea of Shakespeare, attributed to Lee, has any hold on the public mind. Further, I find no evidence in Lee's book that the image as presented by Mr. Wilson was in any substantial sense entertained by Lee himself. Incidentally it should be noted that Lee speaks with contempt of the bust ; extravagantly so, in my opinion. In fact, I think that Mr. Wilson here does grave injustice to a book that, with all its faults and limitations, is on the whole the best general survey that we have of Shakespeare and his work. It is far more than the " indispensable reference book of facts " which even Mr. Wilson allows it to be. It is true that Lee overworked his theory as to the impersonal nature of the plays, their insecurity as evidence regarding the poet's personal life, and it is a theory that is especially provoking to Mr. Wilson. I think that in the balance he is right here as against Lee, but the answer to this extremely vexed question is not quite so self-evident as he seems to believe. " Shakespeare led a life of allegory," said Keats, as Mr. Wilson reminds us : " his works are the comments upon it." And yet none knew better than Keats that immediately a generalisation of that kind is made a score of challenging questions insist upon themselves. Mr. Wilson, for example, sees in Shakespeare's great tragic period the reflection of his personal response to the national depression into which the Elizabethan glory dwindled with the catastrophe of Essex. This, on the other hand, is how Lee accounts for it :

" With his advance in years there came in comedy and tragedy alike a larger grasp of life, a firmer style, a richer thought. Ulti-mately, tragedy rather than comedy gave him the requisite scope for the full exercise of his matured endowments. . . . To seek in the necessarily narrow range of his personal experience the key to Shakespeare's triumphant conquest of the topmost peaks of tragedy is to underrate his creative faculty and to disparage the force of its magic.

" In the Elizabethan realm of letters interest combined with instinct to encourage the tragic direction of Shakespeare's dramatic aptitudes. Public taste gave tragedy a supreme place in the theatre. . . . Shakespeare's devotion to tragedy at the zenith of his career finds all the explanation that is needed in the fact that he was a great poet and dramatic artist whose progressive power was in closest touch and surest sympathy with current predilections."

Again, there is, I think, shrewder sense in Mr. Wilson's view, but this is by no means to say that Lee's view is all nonsense. Browning's retort to Wordsworth's assertion that with the sonnets Shakespeare unlocked his heart, " If so, the less Shakespeare he," cannot be dismissed as merely irresponsible.

But even if we allow that Lee had a not very imaginative conception of the origins of poetry, we are still a long way from charging him with insensibility to the beauty of the poetry itself. And his book is in fact constantly alive in a full and generous way to the supreme quality of Shakespeare's poetry. To imply that it is otherwise is, I submit, to wrong him. The passage about Shakespeare's provision for himself and his

daughters is really very inoffensive in its context.
It comes in Lee's consideration of the poet's
closing days, and suggests no more than that, his
work done, his most solid satisfaction was in the
competence that it had brought him. This may
well have been the case, and if it was there is no
need to read into it some cynical trading of
divine genius. Lee certainly had no such intention.

A parting word with Mr. Wilson. He blames
the unfortunate Stratford bust for the general
impression of Shakespeare as " a kind of Grand
Old Man of literature." Here, surely, is another
figure of Mr. Wilson's fancy. Some poets have
suffered this misfortune, but not, I think, Shakespeare. It is difficult to visualise the fiery young
revolutionary who was the progenitor of Fitz-
gerald's Daddy Wordsworth; and the juvenile
Tennyson who scrawled " Byron is dead " on the
Lincolnshire sands is apt to be stifled in the bardic
mantle and beard of Freshwater. But is not the
Shakespeare of popular affection the energetic,
bright-eyed poet of the London playhouses and
Gloriana's court ?

Even the admittedly uninspired bust itself does
not upset me as it seems to upset Mr. Wilson. I
find in it a harmless piece of monumental masonry
with features that do not strikingly resemble the
few affluent and retired butchers whom I happen
to know. On the other hand, it gives me the
impression of being in a clumsy way a faithful

portrait ; an impression which, it may be
remarked in passing, was shared by Ben Jonson,
who knew Shakespeare well. It is rotund and
heavy-jowled, but even poets sometimes go that
way when they are turned fifty, and it is unreasonable to expect reminiscences of flaming youth on
the tomb of middle age. The truth is, I feel, that
Mr. Wilson, misled into thinking that his book,
full of delicate perception and sanity, needed
some prefatory apologia, pressed Sidney Lee and
the Stratford image into a service that they do
not serve.

Shakespeare, then, does not, in my opinion,
need the ministrations of the higher rescue-league.
On the contrary, I think that one of the best
things about popular taste in England is its un-
sophisticated appetite for Shakespeare. The
majority of people may not care about such
things at all, but a very numerous minority reads
Shakespeare with a living interest and without
any misguided notions. The British Empire
Shakespeare Society has three thousand members,
who meet regularly to read and discuss Shakespeare in a perfectly simple way as though it were
a natural and easy thing for English people to do,
which it is. Each week through a long season
annually some three thousand people visit the
Old Vic and Sadler's Wells theatres in London to
see Shakespeare's plays performed, and they have
no dark misgivings in their hearts. The Stratford company draws substantial audiences all

the year round. Any bookseller will tell you that
Shakespeare remains a steady best-seller, and if a
publisher could be given the copyright of any
author, dead or living, Shakespeare would be his
instant choice. These things are significant.
When a great poet, the greatest, enjoys wide and
continued popular esteem in this practical way,
it is a safe deduction that his reputation is in a
thoroughly sound and healthy state. A few im-
pressarios may complain that Shakespeare does
not pay in the theatre, which usually means that
they have been disappointed in their hopes of
making profit at the rate of two or three hundred
pounds a week by the slovenly and vulgar production of one of his plays. The wholesome thing
about Shakespeare's reputation, not only among
his own countrymen, but the world over, is that
it is founded on a genuine appreciation of his
work, unconfused by any problematic issues.
And if bardolatry is to be found at Stratford and
elsewhere, I don't know that it does Shakespeare
or anyone else any harm. I must confess to a
weakness for it myself, and I do not enjoy or understand Shakespeare's work the less for it. In
short, as a people we have no reason to reproach
ourselves about Shakespeare. In other matters
we have. As a people, for example, we have
done next to nothing to deserve Ben Jonson, who
would top the dramatic poets of any other country as Shakespeare tops our own. But by some
fortunate chance our national account with

Shakespeare is a creditable one. The greatness of our greatest Englishman is firmly established in its true colours. The common image of Shakespeare is not a false one.

CHAPTER II

WHO WAS SHAKESPEARE?

A HUNDRED years ago anyone who asked the question: "Who was Shakespeare?" would have been considered mad. There are those who think that of people who ask it to-day; but this is indelicate. All was well until 1848, when, two hundred and thirty-two years after the Stratford actor's death, a United States Consul at Santa Cruz, in a treatise on yachting, suggested that this William Shakespeare was not the author of the plays. Since then a pretty kettle of fish has been frying, and I understand that to date something like a thousand works have been written on the subject. I have not read all of these.

For a long time scholars who alleged that Shakespeare could not have written the plays agreed that Francis Bacon did. Some of the most eminent went beyond this, and asserted that Bacon wrote the greater part of Elizabethan and Jacobean literature. Then Bacon lost ground in favour of other noblemen, until to-day the claimant chiefly supported is Edward Vere, Earl of Oxford. Mr. Percy Allen is his most formidable champion, and if anyone suggests that Mr. Allen is mad, he must allow that it is the madness of much learning. His *Oxford-Shakespeare Case Corroborated*

(1931) presents a maze of argument through which it evidently requires a mind unlike my own to follow him. The plays of Ben Jonson and Shakespeare-Oxford are for him pleasant fields in which at every step he sinks knee-deep in hidden meanings. Readers who are less fortified in zeal than he will find it very exhausting. But Mr. Allen toils in delight, and to call him names does not answer questions.

It all seems to have begun with a suspicion that William did not write the plays rather than that someone else did. In 1856 Miss Delia Bacon expanded the Consul's doubts, but three years later she died insane, having lived to see a Mr. Smith, of London, advance her namesake as a candidate for the vacated honour. His labours were generously supplemented by Mrs. Pott and Mrs. Gallup – the topic seems always to have been congenial to the feminine mind – and later by Mr. Looney. I well remember in my youth being impressed not by the logic, which I could not follow, but by the pertinacity with which a legal gentleman, Sir Edwin Durning Lawrence, carried on the Baconian campaign in a spate of pamphlets and letters to the Press. His evangelical fury would have exalted the Salvation Army.

If you ask an American for his opinion of the negro question he is apt to retort in evasion that there isn't one. It is tempting to treat the Shakespeare question in the same way, but it won't do. It is surprising that such a question should be, but there it is. Much of the evidence on which it is based is silly, but some of it is effective. It has agitated a considerable body of opinion for nearly a century, and it insists on an answer. This, I think, is not very difficult to find.

The Oxonians having, it seems, superseded the Baconians, some examination of Mr. Percy Allen, their major prophet, will serve our turn. Mr. Allen is not furious. On the whole his debating manners, when they are not too severely tested, are good. I have but one fault to find with his temper. He insists on denouncing the orthodox view as inspired by vested interests, as though all of us who hold it had shares in Stratford hotels. This is a tactical error. Very few of us really feel that way about it. If anyone can prove to me that Banbury Cross is a Banbury cake, I am willing to try to eat it, but in the meantime plain common sense will forgive me for continuing to regard it as something which, if it is not precisely a cross, is in any case not edible. Similarly, if Mr. Allen can prove that the celebrated plays were written by the Earl of Oxford, or even by Guy Fawkes, I am ready unreservedly to transfer the veneration that I now feel for William Shakespeare to his vindicated dupe, whoever it may be. But, again, in the meantime I have a natural preference for Shakespeare, whose identity with the dramatist has always seemed to me to be sufficiently established, even more securely than the identity of Banbury Cross with a cross.

Let Mr. Allen, I say, prove his case, and I will wash my hands of William as an impostor. And so, I think I may assert in the name of orthodoxy, say all of us. But he really must prove it. Because, until then, we have one vested interest which does exercise a very strong hold on us, our vested interest in our own intellectual stability. It is a shock to discover that you have, in what you took to be a simple matter of fact, been suffering from hallucinations. If you do discover it, you will, if you are sensible, adjust your mind to the new conditions, but you are going to resist the evidence at every step. It would be pleasanter to be reassured that you had not been suffering from hallucinations after all.

Let us, then, look at Mr. Allen's evidence put in as proof of his Oxford case. It is axiomatic with the anti-Shakespeare school of thought that whoever it was who wrote the plays wrote them secretly, and used Shakespeare's name to cover the deception. I have not read of any plausible reason why this should have been necessary, nor of any plausible way in which it would have been possible. However, this is an indispensable clause in the brief. The claimant usually, indeed apparently always, being a nobleman, it is alleged that an Elizabethan nobleman could not acknowledge the authorship of plays without losing caste, thus endangering his position at court and in

society. Since no nobleman seems to have tried
it, it is at least as likely that no nobleman had the
brains to, as that he would not have done so if
he could. In fact, it is as certain as anything
humanly could be that if one of Elizabeth's
courtiers could have gone to her with *Macbeth*
and *As You Like It* in his pocket, he could have
had anything under the moon for the asking.
The only greater certainty is that no nobleman,
during a long period of years, could have succeeded in putting something over thirty plays
into Shakespeare's pocket without the whole of
London society, which was then a small and
assiduously cultivated hot-bed of gossip where
nobody's business was his own, knowing all about
it.

Oxford, nevertheless says Mr. Allen, wrote the
plays, wrote them secretly, and called them
Shakespeare's without anyone being the wiser.
Not actually without anyone, as it appears that
he received a thousand pounds a year from the
secret service funds for doing it, part of which was
paid as hush money to Shakespeare, and also to
other theatrical folk who were in the dreadful
secret. I will not do Mr. Allen the discourtesy of
saying arbitrarily that this is nonsense, but it
seems to me to show many of the symptoms.

Oxford, however, though compelled to be a
clandestine poet, was not without an author's
pride, and had no intention of allowing his Stratford pigeon to strut down the ages in borrowed

plumes. So, of course, he employed the device that seems to have been an obsession with the Elizabethans in their creative moods ; he larded his work with cyphers that would enable astute readers like Mr. Allen to penetrate the disguise that had been imposed on him, and do poetic justice in the sight of the world. Circumstance conspired with his design. His family name was Vere. And so, whenever he uses words like ever, never, dissever, persevere, forever, Mr. Allen by a small manipulation of type, nevER, is able to proclaim Oxford calling from the page. As it is impossible to make any sustained use of the English language without frequent repetition of words with the V E R sequence, Mr. Allen is able to cite a profusion of these mandates from the Oxford grave.

Thus bad begins and worse remains behind, which always looks to me as though it were not what Hamlet really meant to say. Inconveniently for Mr. Allen's thesis, Edward de Vere the seventeenth earl of Oxford, died in 1604, after which date several of the Shakespearean plays were written. At least one would have supposed that it would be inconvenient ; but it does not embarrass Mr. Allen. Like the undaunted daughters of desire, he goes straight on. The great dramatist known as Shakespeare was dead, but the impostor was still alive. The demand for his plays was insistent, and so a syndicate of unspecified writers was formed to supply new ones

Cs

in imitation of the well-known manner. Mr.
Allen gets over the difficulty regarding *Macbeth*
and *Lear* by assigning them to an earlier date, but
he is left with *Timon, Pericles, Antony and Cleopatra,
Coriolanus, Cymbeline, The Winter's Tale* and *The
Tempest* on his hands. The first and second of these
were written by George Wilkins, one of Shakespeare's fellow actors. *Antony* and *Coriolanus* were
completions by the syndicate of Oxonian drafts.
Cymbeline was an " almost if not quite " spurious
production by the same agency, and *The Winter's
Tale* genuine Oxford only in the pastoral scenes,
which were written more than twenty years before the date of the play's production. Even if
we take a liberal view on questions of divided or
doubtful authorship – as in *Pericles* for example –
all this is pretty staggering ; but Mr. Allen's best
is yet to come. By no ingenuity can he place the
composition of *The Tempest* before the generally
accepted date, 1611. Here then, at last, is a play
that Oxford could not have written. *The Tempest,*
however, is very widely regarded, if it were not
for Mr. Allen we might say universally regarded
as one of Shakespeare's supreme masterpieces, the
fitting close and crown of his dramatic work,
showing the exercise of his genius in serene and
assured development from all that had gone
before. To allow that such a work was achieved
by the syndicate of journeymen without any aid
from the master whom they were impersonating
would obviously be, from Mr. Allen's point of

view, an exceedingly dangerous admission. There
is only one way out of the dilemma, which is to
argue that *The Tempest* is not such a work at all
and Mr. Allen adopts it. Not that he argues much
about it ; he tells us flat. " The vocabulary of
The Tempest is not only the least Shakespearean,
it is also the poorest of all the plays, excepting
only, perhaps, *Pericles* and *Cymbeline*." Since the
diction is the very life blood of Shakespeare's
work, this can only mean that the play itself is one
of his poorest. Mr. Allen gives a further turn to
his screw, which he must pardon us for calling
a loose one : " there follows the world-famous
speech [Our revels now are ended], wholly un-
Shakespearean in character." *The Tempest*, however, although it was a poor play, was, we learn,
a very subtle and learned allegory on the subject
of " initiation." Its " intimacy and depth of
classical erudition " reveals a mind " soaked in
knowledge of the ancient world." And so – can
it be as a graceful concession to the enthusiasts
whose idol he is replacing by his own Oxford ? –
he gives this one play to Francis Bacon. At this
point in his book Mr. Allen has fought a long and
strenuous fight, but this looks to me uncommonly
like throwing up the sponge.

It would be unfair to give the impression that
Mr. Allen carries on like this all the time, but a
method that falls into such extravagance puts a
severe strain on indulgence. These fanaticisms
apart, Mr. Allen applies to his task an industry

and a courage that it is impossible not to admire.
Further, in his formidable display of textual evidence, he exhibits many passages of which the
solution is obscure, even though we cannot accept
those with which he challenges us. If we could
allow his case any basic probability, we might
find much satisfaction in his exhaustive, not to say
exhausting presentation of it. As it is, we do not
feel it necessary to examine the body of his evidence in detail. I have drawn attention to some of
Mr. Allen's more fantastic arguments because in
kind they are characteristic of the anti-Shake-
speareans in general. Before undertaking the
further responsibility of debating his conclusions
step by step through their labyrinthine progress,
I should have to be convinced either that there
was sufficient evidence to show that William
Shakespeare could not have written the plays, or
that there was not sufficient evidence to show that
he did. I think that there is no evidence in the
one case, and ample evidence in the other. Mr.
Allen, and those of his persuasion, think that
there is ample evidence of Shakespeare's in-
ability to write the plays, and so consider themselves under no serious obligation to examine the
evidence that he did. This is the starting point
always of their attributions, whether to Bacon or
Oxford or another.

Their contention is that William Shakespeare of
Stratford was an illiterate clown, with no more
than a rustic or plebeian experience of life, and

that the plays utterly transcend his scope in their range of knowledge, breeding, and scholarship. Shakespeare's father was a middle-class citizen of sufficient means to give his sons the grammar-school education that was of a rather liberal standard, and although Lee's assumption that William went to the school at Stratford is not supported by any documentary evidence, it is a safe guess to the point of certainty that the boy went to London with so much of book-learning at least. With it, and the genius that informed his plays, his achievement is no matter for surprise. We may go beyond this and confidently assert that without any such education at all, the genius was capable of all that the plays contain. One of the symptoms of genius is an immense capacity for absorbing essential knowledge from every kind of contact. A genius so swift and abundant as this man's could not move about his daily business in the English countryside, the theatres and taverns of London, the great houses and the court where he went mumming, without accumulating more than enough to supply all his creative needs. There is nothing in the plays that would not be easily within the resources of such acquisition. The talk about special knowledge of the law and what not is rubbish. Every dramatist of any account shows in his plays what appears to be expert knowledge of subjects on which he is not an expert at all. The works of Mr. Shaw and Mr. Galsworthy and Mr Granville-Barker and

Mr. Ervine are littered with legal, scientific, economic and martial allusions that indicate not specialist knowledge but the ordinary exercise of quick-witted minds in the common ways of conversation and reading. If I may be excused for the personal example, when I wrote a play about Abraham Lincoln I was congratulated by hundreds – literally – of Americans on my intimate knowledge of their history and national character. At the time when I wrote the play, I had read two or three books on the civil war between the North and South, one life of Lincoln, I had never been to the United States, and I had no American friends. This line of argument about Shakespeare simply has no pertinence. It would be possible to demonstrate by it that the plays could not have been written by anyone.

" I hold it," says Mr. Allen, " to be an unanswerable fact, that no man, however highly endowed, ever can write, or ever did write, outside the basic experiences of his own life." But what are basic experiences ? Oxford, we are told, " was bred in the purple," whereas William Shakespeare was bred in a tradesman's shop. And so the plays, revealing " the most perfect ease and familiarity " among the rank and fashion of the age, were written by Oxford and not by Shakespeare, who lacked the necessary " basic experience." Mr. Dover Wilson has, in fact, made out a very likely case for the supposition that Shakespeare was for some time in the household of his patron, the young Earl of Southampton, on intimate terms, where he would have enjoyed enough basic experience of this kind to satisfy even Mr. Allen. There is, however, no proof of this, and again for the present purpose we do not need it. There is not a scene in the plays that shows a social knowledge beyond the opportunities that Shakespeare of the playhouses must have enjoyed. And as for the history of Courts and Kings, this clearly was accessible to anyone who had a few books, with Holinshed and North's Plutarch among them, within reach. The plain and inescapable truth is that the only special qualification for writing Shakespeare's plays was Shakespeare's genius, and there is no foundation whatever for attributing this to Bacon or Oxford or any man in dispossession of the Stratfordian.

It may be positively asserted, then, that William Shakespeare could have written the plays associated by unbroken tradition with his name. To dispute this is to betray an incapacity for understanding the elementary psychology of genius. Poetry will not submit to conditions such as are here proposed. With so much established, we may look at the evidence that Shakespeare not only could have written but did write the plays.

CHAPTER III

SHAKESPEARE

WILLIAM SHAKESPEARE of Stratford-on-Avon died in 1616 at the age of fifty-three, as is attested by the records of Holy Trinity Church in that town. It has not yet occurred to anyone to dispute the identity of this person with the actor and shareholder of the Globe and Blackfriars theatres in London, James the First's King's Player, and the man who was reported, whether honestly or by fraud, to have written the plays. Several of these were published in quarto form during his lifetime, but they were mostly issued without authority, and even the appearance of his name on some of the title-pages is not important as evidence of his authorship.

In 1623, however, appeared the folio edition of Mr. William Shakespeare's Comedies, Histories, and Tragedies, a work of gigantic achievement. It was published at a pound, and is now worth more. It contained thirty-six plays, twenty of which had not been previously printed. The obligation of the world to the men who undertook this venture cannot, therefore, be measured. The book is, further, sufficient testimony in itself to the plain fact that its author was none other than he who was designated in the title.

The sponsors of the book were John Heminge, who died in 1630, and Henry Condell, who died in 1627. Their birth dates are uncertain. Lee thinks that Edward Blount, one of the five printers or booksellers associated in the enterprise, was chiefly responsible for the editorial work, but Heminge and Condell were the principals in the publication. They had both been fellow actors and shareholders with Shakespeare at the Globe and Blackfriars theatres, both had in addition taken a leading part in the business management of the company, both had been King's Players with him under James, and each had been left the sum of twenty-six shillings and eightpence in Shakespeare's will for the purchase of a memorial ring. These men, in other words, had maintained the closest personal and professional relations with Shakespeare through the greater part of his theatrical career. No one knew the Stratford actor on more intimate terms than they.

These men jointly signed two prefaces to the folio, one in dedication to the brothers William and Philip Herbert, Earls of Pembroke and Montgomery respectively, the other an address to the Great Variety of Readers. It has been suggested that they did not actually write these themselves, but employed someone with a more tutored pen, possibly Blount, to do this for them. The supposition seems a gratuitous one. In any case Heminge and Condell assumed full responsibility for any statements that the prefaces contained by setting their names to them. They were both men of substantial standing, high in their profession, churchwardens of St. Mary Aldermanbury, and there can be no serious question of any equivocation perpetrated under their joint names.

In the dedication the following words appear : " We have but collected them [the plays], and done an office to the dead, to procure his orphans guardians : without ambition either of self profit or fame, only to keep the memory of so worthy a friend and fellow alive, as was our Shakespeare . . ." It is inconceivable that Shakespeare could have practised a stupendous and sustained fraud in the working affairs of the theatres in which he was associated with these men as managers and have kept them in ignorance of it. It is equally inconceivable that they, knowing of the deception, could have published those words attributing the plays to their friend and fellow, Shakespeare. The contention that they spoke of Oxford to the Herberts, who must as certainly have known of the fraud if it had been committed, as their " friend and fellow . . . Shakespeare " is nothing less than farcical.

But if even more conclusive evidence in the matter be desired, the folio supplies it. The prefaces are followed by four poems in praise of the author, the first of them by Ben Jonson, who signs it. The heading reads, " To the Memory of my Beloved, the Authour, Mr. William Shakespeare :

and what he hath left us." If it is idle to
suggest that Heminge and Condell lent themselves to the alleged deception, it is idler still to
suggest that Jonson did ; nor is there any likelier
chance of his having himself been deceived. If
anyone believes that in a matter of such cardinal
importance in the theatre of his time Jonson
can have been fooled for thirty years and more,
he is, as Matthew Arnold said on another occasion, capable of believing anything. And Jonson
calls the Authour his beloved Mr. William Shakespeare. He also, in the poem itself, calls him
" Sweet Swan of Avon." Even if the Baconians
or Oxonians can persuade themselves that Jonson
in using the name William Shakespeare was
merely conniving at the common substitution of
it for that of Bacon or Oxford, they may be
defied to explain why he should call either Bacon
or Oxford a Swan of Avon. Adding proof to
proof, Leonard Digges, another of the folio's
elegiac poets, writes :

> *When that stone is rent,*
> *And time dissolves thy Stratford monument,*
> *Here we alive shall view thee still.*

The evidence of the folio, in short, is decisive.
It adds to our conviction that William Shakespeare of Stratford could have written the plays
the certainty that he did. In face of this, we can
be excused from examining in all their chaotic
detail the attempts to confer this unparalleled

honour on someone else. We may now proceed
to a simple summary of the known facts of Shakespeare's life, in the course of which incidental
corroborations of his authorship will appear.

William Shakespeare was born at Stratford-on-
Avon, in Warwickshire, in April 1564. His
baptismal entry in the register of Holy Trinity
Church is dated the 26th of that month, and a
generally accepted tradition assigns his birth to
the 23rd.

The name, Shakespeare, spelt, as was usual
with nomenclature in those times, in a variety of
ways, was a not uncommon one, and several
Warwickshire families, mostly of the upper
yeoman class, bore it. From one of these, living
at Snitterfield, a Warwickshire village, John
Shakespeare went as a young man to make a
living at Stratford, and some six years later,
probably in 1557, he married Mary Arden, the
daughter of another Warwickshire family of his
own class, living at Wilmcote. Two daughters
died in infancy, and then, in 1564, their third
child was born. They called him William. His
birthplace was in Henley Street.

There are no authoritative records of the poet's
boyhood. During that period his father was
prosperous in trade, dealing in agricultural
products, " corn, wool, malt, meat, skins and
leather " according to Lee's inventory. He
became an alderman when his son was a year old,
and in his office took part three years later in

civic receptions of two companies of players, the Queen's and the Earl of Worcester's, who visited Stratford on their provincial tours. Six years later he served a term as chief alderman, and had now acquired the dignity of being designated as " Mr." in the corporation records. In 1575, by which time his son William was eleven, he was in a position to buy two houses in the town, having already inherited property at Snitterfield from his father, but from that date his fortune suffered a decline, and by 1586 he was being pressed by a creditor who complained in court that the defendant had no goods that could be distrained. In spite of difficulties, however, he managed to keep his home together, and by the time that this public misfortune befell him, and neglect of council business resulted in his removal from the body of aldermen, his son had reached manhood, married, and left for London.

The registers of the Stratford Grammar School, if any were kept at the time of Shakespeare's boyhood, have disappeared. If they could be recovered, it is probable almost to the degree of certainty that they would be found to include the names of John Shakespeare's sons. William, born in 1564, was followed by Gilbert, 1566, Richard, 1573, and Edmund, 1580, all of whom grew up. As the sons of a Stratford burgess, they were entitled to free education at the town school. Boys began their education young, and although at the date when William and Gilbert first went

to school their father was not in need of such
relief, he can scarcely have failed to follow the
example of other leading citizens in making use of
the obvious means to his hand. When the turn
of the younger brothers came, the straitened
resources of the family would make the privilege
a timely one. It is no more than conjecture that
William Shakespeare was in fact educated at the
Stratford Grammar School, but it is conjecture
that has every reason in its favour and none
against it.

Concerning another feature of his boyhood, all
conjecture is unnecessary. Shakespeare's early
years were spent in a thriving country town, and
among the scenes of a pastoral landscape that is
as intimately lovely as any in England. Stratford,
with its two thousand inhabitants, was then about
a fifth of its present size, but there is no difficulty
in realising the nature of its life. Weavers,
malsters, wool-staplers, millers, tanners, dealt
profitably in the products of the surrounding
countryside; with the smaller fry of tradesmen
and "rude mechanicals," the tailors, smiths,
joiners, tinkers, masons, taking more modest
returns from the industry of the town. The few
professional men, notaries, surgeons, pedagogues
and clerics were but little removed by class
consciousness from their neighbours. The pro-
prietors of the great houses in the neighbourhood,
such as the Lucys of Charlecote, were not conspic-
uous in the town life; neither were the illiterate

peasants who were mostly to be found among the
outlying farms and small holdings. The population of the town was essentially a blend of yeoman
and middle-class in character, with a strong fusion
of rusticity in its urban habits. The word that
most exactly fits it is racy. At the time of Shakespeare's birth it seems that the community was
suffering from a mild industrial depression, from
which it never wholly recovered during his life-
time. Local production was not keeping pace
with the trade in imported goods. During the
same period the little town was stricken by severe
visitations of the plague. These are conditions
that display human nature in the rough, its cunning and its generosities alike. Here was a good
average of English character, neither exalted nor
debased, not reduced to ugliness by adversity, but
kept taut by circumstance. A boy with his wits
about him would find in it rare material on which
to sharpen them.

The influence of this early environment on
Shakespeare's work was profound. When he
came to his creative power, his vision was com-
pleter, perhaps, than that of any other dramatic
poet in the history of the world. This is a
commonplace of criticism. His sympathy was
more extensive and his capacity for seeing all
round the figures of his invention acuter than
those of his most highly gifted rivals. The
distinctions between the multifarious people of
his theatre are unfailing in their precision ; even

his tiny fugitive characters assert themselves against each other with a contrast that is as brilliant as the tones are subtle. In the art of escaping from himself into the life of his characters he is the unrivalled master. That is why great caution is necessary in any attempt to invest his plays with autobiographical significance. No one can suppose that they were devoid of this ; but it is dangerous to be sure that we have him, here or there. There is no turn where in this matter he may not deceive us. The intensity of his power for wholly disinterested creation is such that no personal mood can be sure at any moment of holding him against the demands of the life that he is creating.

His integrity as a dramatic artist is, then, less open to question than any other man's. Certainly he can be identified with none of his characters ; and it is rash even to identify him with any of their moments. But in one respect he leaves his mark strongly impressed upon the whole cosmic world that he brought into being. I am not speaking of his natural greatness, of the incomparable imaginative power that he commanded. Certainly this marks his work, as Jonson puts it, for all time, but the proverb is something musty. What I have in mind is a quality that pervades his plays, and had its origins in the environment of his early Stratford days. If we can nowhere say authoritatively – " there – that is Shakespeare speaking for himself," we are constantly aware of

a certain habit that accents his work through and
through. It is the habit of seeing life, the vast
life of his dramatic invention, a little modulated
to the terms of the life that he shared as a youth
in Stratford. The point must not be over-stressed,
but it is, I think, an essential one. There is not
only in his humble folk, the tapsters, clowns,
pike-trailers, shepherds, artisans, gardeners,
serving-men, bawds, hucksters and homespuns
generally, but also in his great personages, the
peers and princes and kings, a savour of homely
wisdom, a pith, a robust humour, a tender
gravity – in short, a raciness, that to my mind
unmistakably reflects the humanity with which
he was early familiar in his native town. Without
his genius, such experience would have gone for
nothing ; but with it, we should have expected
just such experience to have just this influence on
his work. Given the genius, the plays, far from
being the sort that such a man as Shakespeare
could not write, are in this respect impressively
the sort that he would. We here have internal
evidence of Shakespeare's authorship lending, if
it were needed, strong support to the external.

Similarly, in the landscape of his plays Shakespeare is true to his Stratford associations. He
can serve his dramatic purposes with battlefields,
storm-wrack, blasted heaths, Dover cliffs, the
bleak battlements of Elsinore, and, deeply practised in the technical necessities of his stage, he
can place these and a hundred other diverse
Ds

pictures instantly before us with a few deft strokes
of his verbal mastery. But who can read or hear
the plays and be in doubt for a moment as to
where in this respect his heart is ? He can at will
call up any scene that his action demands, but
the scenery that he loves and over which he lingers
time and again is the actual though enchanted
Arden of his boyhood. The sheepfolds, the spring
flowers, the icicles, the mossy banks, the pebbled
brooks, the pastures and woodlands, that in play
after play transcend the mere uses of stagecraft
and become a living organism in the drama, are
pure Warwickshire landscape. It is all trans-
figured into something new and strange by the
exquisite light of his verse, but it is the scene to
which he was bred. Again the creation accords
perfectly with our knowledge of the creator.

In 1582, his nineteenth year, Shakespeare
married Anne Hathaway, a young woman eight
years older than himself, from Shottery, a hamlet
lying a few fields away from Stratford. The
registration of the marriage has not been discovered, but a deed in the Worcester diocesan
records establishes the event. The first child,
Susanna, was born six months later. This was in
May, 1583. In February 1585, twins were born,
a boy and a girl, Hamnet and Judith. Hamnet
died when he was eleven, and Judith, like her
sister Susanna, survived her father by many
years. To be exact, she died in Stratford in 1661
at the age of seventy-six ; Susanna died, also at

Stratford, in 1649, aged sixty-six. Anne, their mother, died in 1623, the year of the Folio publication, at the age of sixty-seven. The celebrated fact that the poet in his will left her only his second-best bed signifies nothing. The will indicates clearly enough that when he died he was on good terms with his family, and since his widow's death occurred at New Place, his own Stratford residence during his retirement, it is a reasonable surmise that he had made other than testamentary provision for her.

This bare recital tells all that is known of Shakespeare's marriage. His wife was of his own class, but nothing is recorded of her character or personality. In 1592, Robert Greene, a playwright whose luck was out, referred in his *Groatsworth of Wit bought with a Million of Repentance* to one who was " in his own conceit the only Shake-scene in a country." The context and occasion leave no doubt as to the identity of the poet lightly disguised under the punning name, and this is the first known authoritative reference to Shakespeare apart from the ecclesiastical records. Spenser's fancied allusion to the dramatist in " Our pleasant Willy " of *The Teares of the Muses* (1591) bears no examination. John Aubrey, however, in his *Brief Lives*, compiled in the later part of the seventeenth century, wrote: " This Wm. [Shakespeare] being inclined naturally to poetry and acting, came to London, I guess about 18, and was an actor at one of the

play-houses, and did act exceedingly well."
Aubrey was a careful gleaner of contemporary
gossip, and the tradition that Shakespeare left
Stratford for London not, indeed, when he was
eighteen, but not later than 1586, when he was
twenty-two, came to be generally accepted. It is
supported by Greene's attack. He calls Shake-
scene "an absolute *Johannes Factotum*," who
"supposes he is as well able to bombast out a
blank verse as the best of you." This clearly has a
two-fold significance. Shakespeare was already
known as a writer of his own or a mender of other
men's plays, and he was of sufficient importance
in that calling to excite the public spleen of an
eminent rival. Such a position is not achieved
in a twelve-month, and that Shakespeare held it in
1592 lends reasonable probability to the tradition
that he was doing 'prentice work in the theatre
not later than 1586. There is nothing to suggest
that his wife accompanied him to London; on the
other hand, there is nothing to prove that she
didn't. Speculation about his married life is
profitless, though Lee, perhaps, does not much
exceed discretion in observing that "Anne
Hathaway's greater burden of years and the like-
lihood that the poet was forced into marrying her
by her friends were not circumstances of happy
augury."

In 1593 Shakespeare published *Venus and Adonis*,
and *Lucrece* in 1594. The printer in each case was
Richard Field, who was born at Stratford in the

same year as the poet, and went to London to learn his trade at the age of fifteen. Both poems were dedicated to Henry Wriothesley, the third Earl of Southampton, then a young man of twenty, and already an admired figure at Elizabeth's court, in terms that indicate high and even affectionate mutual esteem between the poet and his patron. Of his plays no earlier edition has been found than the surreptitious quartos of *Romeo and Juliet* and the two *Richards* in 1597, but by that date he had a stout list of productions in the theatre to his credit. The first of these, *Love's Labour's Lost* in 1591, was followed in rapid succession by *The Two Gentlemen of Verona* (1591), *Comedy of Errors* (1592), *Romeo and Juliet* (1592), *Richard III* (1593), *Richard II* (1593), the disputed *Titus Andronicus* (1593), *The Merchant of Venice* (1594), *King John* (1594), *Midsummer Night's Dream* (1594–5), *All's Well That Ends Well* (1595), *The Taming of the Shrew* (1595), *Henry IV, Parts I and II* (1597) and *The Merry Wives of Windsor* (1597). To these must be added his share in the three parts of *Henry VI* (1592). The exact chronology of these, as of the later plays, remains partly speculative, but future discoveries are not likely to make any material readjustment of the now generally accepted sequence.

In 1596 Shakespeare was living in Southwark. He moved thither from Bishopsgate, the revenue collector of that district, as is shown by a note in the Record Office, obtaining leave to lodge a claim against the poet at his new address for arrears of taxes. In the same year John Shakespeare of Stratford applied successfully to the College of Heralds for a coat of arms, the grant being for " Gold on a bend sable a spear of the first, the point steeled, proper ; and for his crest or cognizance, a falcon, his wings displayed, argent, standing on a wreath of his colors, supporting a spear gold steeled as aforesaid, set upon a helmett with mantels and tassels as hath been accustomed and more plainly appeareth depicted in this margin." The motto was "Non Sans Droict." A year later William bought New Place, the largest house, it is said, in Stratford, at a cost of sixty pounds, then a substantial purchase money. Lee, on a close investigation, estimates that his income up to that time had for some years been not less than a hundred and fifty pounds annually, computed as the equivalent of five times that sum to-day. This, as Lee adds, would be regarded as affluence by the people of Stratford, and when their fellow-townsman became the master of New Place, even only as an occasional visitor from his triumphs in London, he acquired great influence and prestige among them. The author of *Richard II* and *Midsummer Night's Dream* had, it appeared, something in him after all. He soon learned that there were many cases in the town highly meriting his assistance.

New Place, when Shakespeare bought it, was in a state of disrepair, and involved him in

considerable further expenditure. He was, however, in a position to do the thing handsomely. A
popular tradition asserts that Southampton made
him a present of a thousand pounds. There is
nothing inherently improbable in the story, large
as the amount may be. Southampton had the
reputation for liberal, even lavish patronage, and
his favours were much coveted by the poets of the
day. He was, moreover, a man of taste, reserved
in his approval. He must have known that the
homage of Shakespeare was an honour of a very
unusual kind, and he was not likely to under-
value it, even in the material recognition that it
was the patron's customary part to make. The
heightened tone of the *Lucrece* dedication following that of *Venus and Adonis* speaks plainly of the
encouragement that the young nobleman had
given to the poet's friendly advances. He was
rich, and if he had a mind to pay William Shakespeare for his poetry, he could afford to do it well.
A thousand pounds was, perhaps, payment at an
uncommon rate, but then Shakespeare was an
uncommon poet, and Southampton knew it. It
would not be in the least surprising to find the
tradition verified.

Such a gift would have made all easy, but even
without it Shakespeare would have been equal to
the demands of his new Stratford property. In
1599 he became a shareholder in the Globe
Theatre, and from that time added to his earn-
ings as actor and playwright a part of the profits

made by the house. Lee assesses his share, at first
a tenth and later a smaller proportion of larger
returns, as averaging a hundred and fifty pounds
a year. Thus, at the time when he was restoring
the fabric of his new house, beautifying the
gardens and laying out a fine orchard, his income was doubled. He was now by our standards
a fifteen hundred a year man, most of which an
ingenuous government left intact for his own uses.
In 1613 this was further augmented by part
ownership of the Blackfriars Theatre. In 1601,
on his father's death, he inherited the Henley
Street property, where he had been born. In
1602 he bought a plot of land over a hundred
acres in extent, outside Stratford, acquiring a
further twenty acres at a later date.

The records of a lawsuit in 1612, discovered by
Dr. Wallace in 1910, have been accepted by Mr.
Pierce Butler, in his valuable and usually very
cautious *Materials, etc.*, already cited, as proving
that Shakespeare in 1604 and for some years about
that date was living with a family named Mount-
joy in Silver Street, Cheapside. I see nothing in
the papers to support this. Shakespeare, by the
testimony of one witness, " laye in the house,"
but whether once as a visitor or as a lodger or
part tenant there is nothing to show. So far as
they throw any light on the question, the depo-
sitions – Shakespeare himself was a witness – seem
to me to discredit the theory of permanent
residence in Silver Street. Somewhere in London,

however, he lived until 1611, when he retired to
Stratford. In the meantime, amid an intense
theatrical activity, he kept close watch on his
interests in his native town. More than once he
appeared in the local court as plaintiff for the
recovery of debts, sometimes of a disconcertingly
trivial character. In 1604 Shakespeare produced
Othello and *Measure for Measure* ; in the same year
he sued a Stratford apothecary for one pound
fifteen shillings and tenpence. It should be added
that petty litigation of this sort was a bad habit
of the time, and further that Shakespeare seems
to have lent small sums freely, no doubt with
discouraging results. Perhaps it merely was that
now and then an impostor found that even the
gentle Shakespeare could be imposed upon once
too often.

Throughout these years Shakespeare's fertility
as a dramatist was prodigious. Between *The
Merry Wives* in 1597 and the end of his known
career fourteen years later he produced seventeen plays, excluding *Pericles*. And what plays ;
the power and pressure, the physical size of them.
A list of their names alone has a titanic ring :

> *Henry V* (1598)
> *Much Ado About Nothing* (1599)
> *As You Like It* (1599)
> *Twelfth Night* (1600)
> *Julius Cæsar* (1600)
> *Hamlet* (1602)

Troilus and Cressida (1603)
Othello (1604)
Measure for Measure (1604)
Macbeth (1606)
King Lear (1607)
Timon of Athens (1608)
Antony and Cleopatra (1608)
Coriolanus (1609)
Cymbeline (1610)
The Winter's Tale (1611)
The Tempest (1611).

At first, it sounds incredible, and then, on reflection, the wonder of it becomes rational. Again, the genius has to be predicated, that genius which swept up and embodied the extraordinary vigour of Elizabethan England. Without it, no conditions could have produced such results, but with it, the conditions were supremely favourable. Aubrey had been told that Shakespeare was " the more to be admired " because he " was not a company keeper . . . would not be debauched, and if invited to, writ : he was in pain." In other words, Shakespeare nursed energies that by nature were prodigious. He was not embarrassed by material troubles. He was working in theatres that would perform his plays as a matter of course as soon as they were written. His audience had a vigour that matched his own, and could respond to it. A highly intelligent court was eager to applaud him. He was sure of popular suffrage for the best that he could do ; the topmost flights of poetry were not above the understanding of a crowd that loved great rhetoric and was not abashed by beauty. Every encouragement that could be desired by the impatience of genius was his abundantly. He was not a poet of remote and experimental vision fighting a difficult cause. He was the poet for whom an age already accustomed to heroic action and heroic verse had been waiting. He had no way to make against the chill winds of stupidity and indifference. Everywhere about him were benign influences urging him to go forward. With a capacity for personal suffering as great as any man's in history, he must nevertheless have experienced throughout his twenty years of crowded creation an unexampled happiness. In an exaltation such as this, the process at once of incomparable power and incomparably fortunate circumstance, even that unexampled wealth of invention no longer seems miraculous. As we contemplate the phenomenon, slowly we begin to see it shaping as he saw it, without fuss or tiresome introspection. He had a job to do in the theatre, and he did it. That it happened to be the greatest job, perhaps, that ever had been or would be done in the theatre or out of it was a consideration for which he had no time to spare. But here was a zest in which the human mind has never made a nearer approach to divinity.

What happened to Shakespeare between 1611 and his death in 1616 nobody knows. If he wrote anything in those years, it has not survived. For myself, I find it impossible to believe that he wrote nothing. Prospero in *The Tempest* might break his wand, but a gift such as Shakespeare's is not suddenly to be stilled like that. There is nothing to suggest that he suffered any incapacitating illness ; and short of that he can hardly have suffered a total loss of inspiration. Something, a good deal, may be allowed for the exhaustion following those twenty burning years, but in the congenial seclusion of Stratford recovery would have been rapid. It may well be that he wrote no more for the theatre, but it is against all probability that he wrote no more verse. In 1611 he was forty-seven years of age. The last five years are reputed to have been years of domestic peace and pleasant social contacts. What appears to me to be the most important and the safest conjecture about Shakespeare's life is that they also witnessed an Indian summer of lyric or narrative verse, the old spontaneity shining again through the perfected experience of his art. If so, what verse it must have been.

He died in 1616, on his birthday, April 23rd. It is the date of Wordsworth's death : also of Rupert Brooke's. It is St. George's Day. His will, made shortly before his death and preserved at Somerset House, tells us much of interest about his family affairs. The first bequest is of a hundred and fifty pounds to his younger daughter, Judith, who in her thirty-second year had recently married Thomas Quiney, the son of a Stratford mercer and four years her junior. He was a vintner, but not for long a prosperous one. He subsequently departed from Stratford in poverty, apparently leaving his wife behind him. Judith was to receive a further hundred and fifty pounds if she was still living " at the end of three years next ensuing the day of the date of this my will," which she was. To his sister Johanna (Joan), who had married William Hart, a hatter, Shakespeare left twenty pounds, and possession for life, at an annual rental of twelve pence, of the family premises in Henley Street, where she had been living since her father's death in 1601. Her husband died but a few days before her brother, the next provision in whose will is for the payment of five pounds to each of her three sons.

To his elder daughter, Susanna Hall, Shakespeare left New Place, the Henley Street houses in reversion, the rest of his Warwickshire property, and his interest in the Blackfriars Theatre. This bequest was entailed in the male line, failing which Elizabeth Hall, Susanna's daughter, was to inherit. To this Elizabeth he left all his plate, except his " broad silver and gilt bowl," which went to his daughter Judith. The rest of his " household stuff whatsoever " he left to Susanna and her husband, John Hall, a Stratford doctor of high standing, who were made joint executors

of the will. Smaller bequests, in addition to the
" second-best bed with the furniture " to his wife,
were ten pounds to the poor of Stratford, five to
Thomas Russell, thirteen pounds six shillings and
eightpence to Francis Collins, twenty shillings to
a godson, William Walker, " my sword " to
Thomas Combe, twenty-six shillings and eightpence apiece to four Stratford friends " to buy
them rings," and the same to " my fellows "
John Heminge, Richard Burbage, and Henry
Condell, the actors with whom he had told an
imperishable tale.

Susanna Hall moved with her husband to New
Place on her father's death, from their residence
which is still known in Stratford as Hall's Croft.
Her mother, the Anne Hathaway whose name
is a strangely remote evocation in Shakespeare's
story, seems to have lived with them, since it was
there that she died in 1623. Neither Susanna nor
Judith had sons who survived them, and Elizabeth Hall became her grandfather's heiress. In
1626, when she was eighteen, she married Thomas
Nash, a young Stratford man of property, and
shortly after his death in 1647, became the wife
of John Barnard, a widower with an estate in
Northamptonshire. He was created a baronet
by Charles II. By neither marriage did Susanna
have children, and with her death as Lady
Barnard in 1669 Shakespeare's direct line came
to an end.

The poet was buried in Holy Trinity, the

Stratford church where he had been baptised. The famous and exasperating monument, designed and executed by a Southwark mason named Janssen or Johnson, was erected some four years later.

CHAPTER IV

REPUTATION

It may safely be said that Shakespeare to-day is the most famous writer in the world. Moreover, there is hardly to be found a critic of any authority who would dispute that, all things considered, he is the greatest. Between his death and the present time his fame has experienced many fluctuations, but it is now established on a basis from which it is not likely ever to be shaken. The habit of blind acceptance that refuses to see his perfection marred by any blemish, once threatened to become fashionable; it is no longer in favour, but also we are no longer likely to make fools of ourselves by condescending to Shakespeare in the manner of the late seventeenth century and the eighteenth. This is the place, however, to consider, not Shakespeare's posthumous reputation, but the esteem that he and his work enjoyed during his life-time.

This, clearly, was very high. Greene in his *Groatsworth* called him " an upstart crow, beautified with our feathers," but this was the jibing of professional jealousy. It is an almost isolated instance of contemporary ill-will towards Shakespeare, and, even so, Henry Chettle, who published Greene's outburst as " written before his

death and published at his dying request," made
a handsome apology a few months later for having printed an attack which had given offence to
one whom he had seen to be in " demeanor no
less civil than he excellent in the quality he pro-
fesses. Besides, divers of worship have reported
his uprightness of dealing, which argues his
honesty, and his facetious grace in writing, that
approves his art." The " civil demeanor " is
confirmed by general testimony. " He was
honest," says Jonson, " and of an open and free
nature." He called him gentle Shakespeare :
" I loved the man, and do honour him, on the
side of Idolatry, as much as any." John Davies,
the Hereford poet, wrote of him in 1603 as having
" wit, courage, good shape, good parts," and as
being " generous in mind and mood." The
Return from Parnassus, dated 1600, makes repeated
references to " sweet Mr. Shakespeare." The
sentiment that pervades contemporary allusions
to the poet is aroused also by his poetry. The
man and his work during his own life-time are
described as friendly, enchanting, mellifluous,
honey-tongued. Francis Meres in 1598, com-
mending him in the famous words, " Shakespeare among the English is most excellent in
both kinds for the stage, for Comedy . . . for
Tragedy . . ." added, " the Muses would speak
with Shakespeare's fine filed phrase, if they
would speak English." He is nowhere saluted as
an innovator or reproached as a rebel. He is

Es

celebrated everywhere as the poet who is doing with supreme grace and ease just what the age most desired a poet to do. The ease, indeed, stuck in Ben's gullet. The passage is familiar, but must not be omitted. " I remember the Players have often mentioned it as an honour to Shakespeare, that in his writing, whatsoever he penned, he never blotted out a line. My answer hath been, would he had blotted a thousand. Which they thought a malevolent speech. I had not told posterity this, but for their ignorance, who choose that circumstance to commend their friend by, wherein he most faulted." No one admired Shakespeare more than Jonson did, or praised him better. It is unlikely that Shakespeare, for his part, was less generous. But on questions of dramatic theory there must have been acute differences of opinion between the two greatest dramatists of their day, differences, we may be sure, that would excite Jonson, with his learning and even pedantry, his insistence on æsthetic principles, a good deal more sharply than they would his tolerant and spacious friend. Thomas Fuller in his *Worthies of England* (1662, but compiled in the 'forties) records in his notice of Shakespeare " the wit-combats between him and Ben Johnson ; which two I behold [Fuller was born in 1608, so is speaking by report] like a Spanish Great Galleon and an English man of war : Master Johnson, like the former, was built far higher in Learning ; solid, but slow in his

performances. Shakespeare, with the English
man of war, lesser in bulk, but lighter in sailing,
could turn with all tides, tack about, and take
advantage of all winds, by the quickness of his
wit and invention." A little over-figured, perhaps, but not far amiss, we feel, in meaning.

Shakespeare, greater than his great rival, was
also more popular. He was the acknowledged
master of his time. The compilers of that living
monument of industry, *The Shakespeare Allusion-
Book*, have recovered from a period of thirty-two
years, 1591–1623, that is to say from the year of
Love's Labour's Lost to that of the first Folio, two
hundred published references, explicit or implied,
to Shakespeare. Times have changed indeed.
That is probably about as many as Mr. Bernard
Shaw gets from his press-cutting agency in a
month. Nevertheless, Shakespeare's record in
publicity is not the less notable of the two. Those
two hundred allusions represent Shakespeare's
generation as bestowing remarkable honour upon
its chosen poet. Almost without exception the
references are eulogistic, or take the form of
borrowings and citations as from an accepted
well-spring of poetry.

The reputation was not only wide, it was also
gracious. There is a friendly note in the simple
words of a bequest made by Augustine Phillips,
a Globe actor who died in 1605, " To my fellowe
William Shakespeare a thirty shilling piece in
gold." When Aubrey was writing, Shakespeare

was still a living memory, and it was of " a handsome, well shaped man : very good company, and
of a very ready and pleasant smooth wit."
Nicholas Rowe, a poet laureate celebrated in one
of Dr. Johnson's best *Lives*, published in 1709 an
edition of Shakespeare's works, which, as Mr.
Pierce Butler points out, has had less than its due
from subsequent criticism. He added to it what
was the first attempt to give a careful summary
of Shakespeare's life, and a very creditable effort
in biography it was. Moreover, it demonstrates
the fact that in the eighteenth century writers of
little or no genius wrote well. Rowe was now
writing within a few years of a century after
Shakespeare's death, and he was able to epitomise
all that tradition had handed down of his author's
character. Later research has done nothing to
modify his conclusion. Shakespeare's " exceed-
ing candour and good nature," he tells us, " must
certainly have inclined all the gentler part of the
world to love him."

Shakespeare's first association with the theatre
was as an actor. It is a mistake, but not an uncommon one, to suppose that this profession was
then of low standing. Many people have a
vague idea that actors were regarded by the law
as rogues and vagabonds. This was the case only
in respect of actors who had not provided themselves with the statutory licence from some person
of accredited rank, which none of the important
companies neglected to do. There was no

difficulty in securing this patronage, which was readily granted by noblemen who by a simple formality could attach to themselves a service very agreeable to their social and artistic tastes. It is true that the public playhouses, in which the licensed companies did most of their work, were at times in disfavour with the civic authorities, and not without reason. At seasons of political unrest they were dangerous centres of intrigue, and disorderly scenes that had not been rehearsed were frequent. Also, at a time when hygiene was undreamt of, they were fertile breeding places of contagion in a city that never knew from week to week when it would next be in the grip of the black death. The constabulary mind of the boroughs was naturally antagonistic, towards an institution that encouraged these menaces and in return did no more than carry on foolish antics that respectable people could very well do without. But the influences opposed to censorship of this nature were powerful. The nobles themselves protected the playhouses ; and, above them, the authority both of Elizabeth and James encouraged the players who at appointed intervals would provide the revels at court. In addition to this advantage, the theatres enjoyed the enthusiastic support of the public. The merchants, men about town, wits and gentlemen, tradesmen and apprentices, looked upon the theatre as a necessary element in civilised life. As in this they were at one with the great personages of the land, even the highest, beadledom was hard put to it to make much way with its policy of discouragement. In crises of disease the theatres could be and were closed by summary edict, but otherwise they flourished. And the actors, most of them amusing and agreeable people of rational habits, were among the most respected and most admired members of the community. When the actor happened also to be the poet of incomparable sonnets, and the dramatist of altogether enchanting plays, his position was one which few could afford not to envy. Shakespeare, we may be sure, was punctilious in the observance of etiquette. Rank was rank, and no man lost his self-respect in recognising it. If a great poet found that his art was pleasurable to the sovereign, he was not going to scout his fortune by putting on airs about it. It would be difficult to imagine a prettier scene than Shakespeare in audience with Elizabeth, a scene that must certainly have an actual if unspecified sanction. The deportment on both sides would be perfect. On such an occasion neither the greatest Queen nor the greatest Poet in history would make any mistake. And if the Queen forgot all about it next day, the Poet would keep his sense of proportion too. Both had their work to do, and neither lacked the full measure of its reward. There can be no doubt to any vivid reconstruction of his age, that Shakespeare was, and knew himself to be, one of its most fortunate masters.

Shakespeare's first employment seems to have been with the Earl of Leicester's men, who had twice visited Stratford during his boyhood, once when he was eight, and again when he was twelve. Kenilworth, Leicester's Warwickshire seat, thirteen miles away, would no doubt be their headquarters on these occasions. Leicester died in 1588, and his company of players had its licence renewed by Lord Strange, afterwards the Earl of Derby. Shakespeare remained with it, and under different patrons was one of its members until the end of his career, as actor, dramatist, shareholder. In 1594 it became part of the Lord Chamberlain's company, then the foremost organisation in the country. In the Christmas of that year he appeared with the Lord Chamberlain's men in two Christmas productions before the Queen, the company receiving thirteen pounds six shillings and eightpence as agreed payment, with a further six pounds thirteen shillings and fourpence as personal bounty from Elizabeth ; twenty pounds in all for the two command performances. In 1598 the company produced Jonson's *Every Man in His Humour* ; according to Rowe, through Shakespeare's intervention. Jonson, it is said, submitted his play – he was then twenty-five years of age, nine years Shakespeare's junior – and it was about to be rejected, " when Shakespeare luckily cast his eye upon it, and

found something so well in it as to engage him
first to read it through, and afterwards to recom-
mend Mr. Johnson and his writings to the public."
The authenticity of the story has been questioned,
but I do not know why Rowe or anyone else
should have fabricated it. In any case Shakespeare himself acted in the play, and his name
appears first in the list of players printed by
Jonson in his own edition of the work. Jonson's
Sejanus (1603), was also produced by the Lord
Chamberlain's men, and again Shakespeare's
name appears as an actor. Rowe states that
" the top of his performance was the ghost in
his own Hamlet," (1602). William Oldys (1696–
1761), the compiler of *The Harleian Miscellany*,
had a story that one of Shakespeare's brothers
used to talk in his old age of William's appearance, wearing a long beard, as Adam in *As You
Like It*. In the Folio of 1623, Heminge and
Condell put Shakespeare's name at the head of
the list of actors in his own plays.

On Elizabeth's death in 1603, Shakespeare's
company became the King's Players under
James, and gave frequent performances at his
court. If the zest of the national life was waning,
the popularity of the actors did not sink, and
one of James I's very few merits was that he
enjoyed the play. Already in Scotland he had
protected a company of visiting players from the
indignation of the Kirk. On the English throne
he indulged his taste freely, the actors being

summoned to court "at least three times as
often," says Lee, "as in the preceding reign."
Shakespeare, during the last eight years of his
professional life, enjoyed everything that the
prestige of his calling could bring him. He was a
principal member of the leading company,
directly under the King's patronage, and he was
its chief dramatist. Well might Thomas Otway
write, in 1680 :

> Our Shakespeare wrote too in an age as blest,
> The happiest poet of his time, and best,
> A gracious Prince's favour cheered his Muse,
> A constant favour he ne'er feared to lose.
> Therefore he wrote with fancy unconfined,
> And thoughts that were immortal as his mind.

To have been the worst of the Stuarts is a melancholy record, but the first James can plead in
mitigation an enthusiasm for William Shakespeare.

The London theatres in which Shakespeare's
company acted were The Theatre and The
Curtain, both in Shoreditch ; The Rose and The
Globe, in Southwark on the south side of the
Thames ; and The Blackfriars, off what is now
Queen Victoria Street. He also played in the
theatre at Newington Butts, and in the inn-
yard of The Crosskeys in Gracechurch Street.
His career began in The Theatre, but his fame
was chiefly established in The Globe and The

Blackfriars. The former was built in 1599, and it was there that most of the company's work was done until 1610, from which date the winter performances took place in the newly reconstructed Blackfriars. The Globe was built on what was known as the " public " model ; the floor of the auditorium was open to the sky. The Blackfriars was a " private " theatre ; the whole building was roofed in. The provision of the one type of house for use on warm sunny days at the riverside, and of the other against the inclemencies of winter, although it was a little discounted by the English climate, was very popular with the patrons of the company. Shakespeare's Globe was burnt down in 1613, the thatched roof taking fire from a mismanaged stage explosion. There was no loss of life, though one spectator had his breeches set alight. A nameless immortal saved the situation by quenching him with a bottle of ale. A new Globe was built in 1614, less than two years before Shakespeare's death. The surmise that Shakespeare periodically went on the provincial tours that his fellows are known to have undertaken is a reasonable one, but supported by no documentary proof.

The performances in which Shakespeare sometimes took part in the Crosskeys inn-yard were a survival of an old custom that began to be superseded by the opening of The Theatre in 1576. This was the first building designed in

England exclusively for the production of plays, and its construction, like that of the other theatres that were rapidly built in and about the city, was directly influenced by the methods to which the players had long been trained in the inn-yards. These yards were open, and surrounded by covered galleries which ran round the internal frontage of the upper stories of the house. Several examples of this architecture may still be seen, the New Inn at Gloucester, the Golden Cross at Oxford, and the George at Huntingdon among others. When a performance was to be given, a platform would be built out into the open yard from a ground floor doorway which was used by the players for their entrances from a room beyond. Part of the audience, the groundlings, assembled in the open yard round the platform, and part found superior accommodation in the galleries. These were the essential features of traditional stage production in the yards, and they were preserved precisely in the new theatres. Small elaborations were made, and a greater efficiency in stage management ensured, but in all radical respects The Theatre and The Globe, in which Shakespeare learnt his mastery as a dramatist, were the natural and in no way complex development of the old machinery. The projecting platform or apron, bringing the players almost toe to toe with part of their audience, open on three sides and with no front curtains ; the entrance doors far up the stage ; and nothing

but the simplest device in shape of a small recess
and balcony at the back to indicate change of
scenes – these were the standardised conditions
under which Shakespeare worked, and they are
of the greatest importance to any consideration
of his art.

It has been a habit of criticism to regard these
conditions as the result of inexperience, for which
in some way allowances have to be made. Lee,
usually so sound in his appraisement of Shakespeare's work, is here a notable offender. His
valuable examination of the Shakespearean
theatre is marred by an undertone of apology,
and he accounts it as an added testimony to the
genius of the poet and his actors that they were
able to create the effect they did with resources so
severely limited. The view is a prevalent one.
We are asked to believe that the Elizabethans and
Jacobeans used the stage they did merely because
they knew no better. This I take to be a gross
misconception.

CHAPTER V

THE first thing that we must realise about Shakespeare's theatre is that it was conditioned by an audience that loved both great poetry and great rhetoric. They wanted their plays in verse, and the verse could be neither too profound nor too swelling for them. The beauty, the fire, the imagery of the word were not agreeable decorations, they were a living element of the drama, almost, one might say, the heart of it. Without these, the action and the scene were nothing ; with them, no improbability of action and no inconsistency of scene could offend. Let the poet keep his word steadily alive with passion, and he was free to suit his own convenience in the rest. For this passion meant essential truth, and the audience knew it. If the poetry was right, then neither idea, which was the principle of tragedy, nor character, which was that of comedy, could be violated. Without a sense of dramatic poetry, no ingenuity can defend the concluding scenes of *The Two Gentlemen of Verona* and *Measure for Measure* ; with it, no defence is necessary. The poet had played out his passion on the stage ; he found himself with an unresolved plot on his hands, and brought it to an arbitrary end, that

was all. To some tastes this is shocking, but it did
not shock the subjects of Eliza and our James.
They knew better than that.

It is aimless to abuse the methods of one age
with those of another. The new-fangled theatre
that took hold of the Restoration had its own
merits, and for good or bad it has influenced the
English stage ever since far more than the
theatre that Shakespeare knew. Personally,
I think it has been for bad rather than good, but
that is at the moment beyond my commission.
The point that I am here concerned to make is
that Shakespeare, if he could have seen the
spectacular triumphs of our modern theatre,
their magnificent *décor*, their brazen frenzy, their
bewitching impudence : if he could have seen the
less intoxicating and less intoxicated masterpieces
of our drawing-room drama, he would have
been stirred to no envy. He would think that he
had fallen back into some age of barbarism.

I would not be misunderstood. There are a
score of dramatists among us to-day, from Mr.
Shaw at seventy odd down to Mr. van Druten
at seventeen odd, whose minds would interest
Shakespeare, and that is praise enough for any
man. But to suppose that Shakespeare, seeing
the methods by which their minds are presented
on the stage, would lament that he had not been
born into this so much more fortunate, more
expert world, is nonsensical. Shakespeare and his
players conceived and presented a drama that has

never been excelled. This implies not only native genius, but supreme executive skill. There was nothing that they wanted to do that they could not do. If the instrument to their hands had been in the smallest degree inadequate to their inexorably urgent purpose they could and would have changed it. It was not ; it was an instrument magnificently equal to every demand that they could make upon it.

Already in the court masques, even in their own court performances, these men could see what another stage technique could do. Inigo Jones was less than ten years younger than Shakespeare. When the players appeared before Elizabeth and James, the methods of The Globe had to be discarded in favour of the paint and paste-board that were esteemed by the masters of the revels. But they took none of these notions back into their theatre. They were loyal subjects, and were willing enough to go monkeying at the royal command, but in the serious business of their art they respected an economy by which alone they could preserve the integrity of their vision. To see Shakespeare's stage as something crude and elementary is not to see it at all. In plain terms of efficiency it was probably, like Shakespeare's Ghost, the top of our performance. It was beautifully sufficient for the greatest drama that the greatest race of dramatists has produced.

Any lack of understanding in this matter must impoverish the performance of Shakespeare's

plays. To hear Hamlet soliloquising in the dim
recesses beyond a proscenium arch is to be assured
that neither producer nor actor knows what he is
about. The sorry make-believe fades into a
vision of Richard Burbage holding his audience
spellbound as he stood above them, under them,
face to face with them in broad sunlight – the
performances were given in the afternoon – not
dreaming in a remote and solitary minor key, but
burning with the still incandescence of great
poetry among the people. No one then in that
theatre lolled back in his seat agreeably bored.
Every man in the place was straining back to the
player, eager with his eagerness, with Shakespeare's.

And so with the whole technique of the plays.
It was evolved in conditions without which it can
never be reproduced. This is no plea for anti-
quarianism in the theatre ; it is a plea for life,
Shakespeare's own life in his own theatre. We
do not need to reconstruct The Globe for the
purpose, but we do need to realise imaginatively
what exactly were the fundamental aspects of
The Globe in action. It is to realise a theatre
in which horseplay, rhetoric, violence have their
place, but a theatre that in its poetry and its
scorn of pictorial triviality is intellectually and
imaginatively pure.

Pure may seem to be an odd word to use of an
art so robust, so voluble, so crowded as was that of
Shakespeare's theatre, but it is, I think, the just

one. When Jonson saluted Shakespeare as " not of an age but for all time " he was saying nothing at variance with Hamlet's own direction to the players that they should " show the very age and body of the time his form and pressure." Jonson was awarding immortality to the heirs of his friend's invention, but none knew better than he that the dramatist must inform his fable, whatever it may be, with the spirit that he has drawn from his own age, or see it fall dead before him on the stage. The spirit and thought and idiom of his time are reflected with an unfailing veracity in Shakespeare's plays, and not less in one than in another. *Lear* and *Antony* are as much the products of Elizabethan England as *The Merry Wives* and *As You Like It*. His theatre was born of an epoch full of onset and stamina, with powerful lungs and an uncommonly strong stomach. These features are inherited by the plays. The first thing that strikes us about these entertainments is their immense staying-power, their fullness, the prodigality of their matter. Here is no pretty carpentry. It is all sledge-hammer stuff, but wrought of a sledge-hammer swung on to anvils of gold by an athlete of the Titans. It is learnt from a large age. And its manner rings with a challenge that such an age could understand. That is what I meant by saying that it was a theatre at once of great poetry and great rhetoric. This lovely verse, charged with all farthest intimations of the human spirit, had to hold the

Fs

attention of men familiar in the taverns and ante-chambers with tales and deeds of fraud and stealth and chartered piracy. In spite of its brutalities it was not a vicious age, and in spite of its emphasis it was not vulgar ; but also it was not an age of suave discretions. In the playhouse you had to speak up to be heard, and Shakespeare's rhetoric, surging abreast with his poetry, was the device that he employed to this end. A magnificent device it was.

But, it might seem, purity is the last thing that could be claimed for an art conforming so freely with these necessities. Nevertheless, there it was, more serenely, I am convinced, than at any time in our theatre. What I have in mind has nothing to do with morals or behaviour ; it is not even concerned with the material of the plays themselves. Decorum no doubt often went by the board on the floor and in the galleries of The Globe, and for all its greatness Shakespeare's drama trailed a good many loose ends on the stage. Neither on the platform nor off it was The Globe a trim and tidy theatre. But in the complex and subtle business of presenting a play at once with the greatest possible economy and the greatest possible effect, I am convinced that it achieved a purity besides which most stage productions would seem to be incurably messy and unkempt. It was not that the stage management was more competent in detail than, say, that of the better type of production in London and New

York to-day ; it could not be that. The excellence
lay in a fixed determination to concentrate on two
things, great drama and great acting, to the relative exclusion of everything else. Our modern
drama has evolved its own methods, and it would
be folly to ask it to employ others. The West End
of the theatre is slick, polished, admirably drilled ;
but, virile and intelligent as it sometimes is, it
seldom escapes wholly from the tyranny of its
devices. Here, during the rehearsals of a fine
play, given adequate time, there usually comes a
day, just before the superficial machinery asserts
itself – the costumes and lighting and scenery and
make-up – when the whole thing suddenly takes
life and displays the long-wooed spirit in being.
Then, for that day, there is a purity that, I think,
is never quite recovered. A crust or film of
pretence seems to settle on it after that, a disguise
that obscures, it may be ever so slightly, the
artistic reality that shone out for a day. When the
curtain goes up the audience has little or no
means of detecting this ; indeed, the players and
the producer themselves are hardly aware of it
any longer. But the purity has, in fact, been
smutched.

On the Bankside it was different. What the
discipline was at rehearsals we cannot tell. If
Hamlet's admonishment to the players not to
mouth it, saw the air, and o'erstep the modesty
of nature may be taken as reflecting Shakespeare's
own experience, and if the stories of comedians

getting the sack for gagging, be true, it appears
that authority was no stricter than it should have
been.   It is reasonably certain, however, that
with men like Burbage and Shakespeare and
Edward Alleyn on the scene these indiscretions
never got beyond control. Bad acting then was
what it is now, and masters such as these were not
likely to tolerate it in any dangerous degree.
They and their principal fellows, it must be
remembered, were shareholders in the theatre,
with a personal stake beyond their wages in its
success, and slackness would inevitably mean the
disapproval of a highly critical audience.   There
is every reason to believe that a company of
players on the Bankside took their work neither
more nor less seriously than a company of players
in the West End. So far they may be considered
as on equal terms.   But then the difference
asserted itself.   Again there came a day when for
the first time *Hamlet* or *Twelfth Night* or *Henry V*
or *Macbeth* took living shape, a thrilling embodi-
ment of the poet's original conception.   And
from that day the glory was never lost. What
remained to be added then before performance
was a firmer grasp of outline, a surer touch in
the cadences, a tightening of the action and
dialogue, a rounder rhetorical attack. Not for a
moment was the hold on that reality slackened.
No considerations were allowed to deflect the
common purpose from essentials to trifles ; there
were, in fact, no trifles to be considered. When

Burbage, in his best Elizabethan dress, had to represent a king, he put a crown on if the fancy pleased him, or appeared without it if not. Someone, no doubt, blew his trumpet at the appointed time, or hung a bush out to denote a tavern. Such a fellow would get his sixpence, and be a nuisance to nobody. But from the moment when the life of the play illuminated a rehearsal, it, and it alone, was the care of the players. That is what is meant by saying that the art of the Shakespearean stage was intellectually and imaginatively pure.

There were three principal ways in which the structure of the playhouse in which Shakespeare worked affected his craftsmanship. It allowed, or rather necessitated the closest possible intimacy of contact between the players and the audience ; it encouraged a multiplicity of scenes, a rapid transition from one place to another, which was indicated in the text and perhaps by the use of one or two properties ; and, as a consequence of this, it facilitated a swift continuity of stage action. The shape and movement of his plays were profoundly influenced by these consider-ations, indeed, they were governed by them, and it is impossible for any production that does not constantly bear them in mind to give an adequate idea of Shakespeare's drama in the theatre.

On the now universally employed proscenium stage an adroit producer can retain much of the rapid movement of Shakespeare's plays by a skilful use of a permanent architecture with drop-scenes or front cloths. It is at best a clumsy substitute for the methods of The Globe, but it serves. The average production at The Old Vic or Stratford, for instance, succeeds in keeping the play afoot at a satisfactory pace, though the elaborate stage machinery that has been installed in the beautiful new Avonside theatre obviously presents dangers that must be watched. I recently saw there a production of *The Merchant of Venice* by M. Komisarjevsky, who elsewhere has done much distinguished work, which indulged in a scenic fantasia that in my opinion left the play stone-dead on the stage. Had Shakespeare been there it would not have been surprising to find him stone-dead too in the audience. Mr. Harcourt Williams and Mr. Bridges Adams, however, to name the two producers at present regularly engaged in presenting Shakespeare, don't make mistakes like this. Their perform-ances are, inevitably, open to criticism, but they do not drag. An Elizabethan crowd might have a good many things to say to these producers, but no occasion for urging them to get on with it.

The multiplicity of scenes used by Shakespeare, treading hard on the heels of another, has some-times been considered to result in formlessness. This, however, is an example of what happens to criticism that measures art by theory instead of deducing theory from art. The only pertinent question about the construction of a play is whether the means that it employs create a meritable effect. If they do, the play is well-constructed, and doctrinaire objections are but a waste of words. It is interesting to note that in our own time the fashion for a clean-cut sequence of three, four, or five acts is being challenged by a return to the much more flexible Shakespearean form, which is, in fact, peculiarly sympathetic to the English mind. It is, moreover, significant that Ben Jonson, steeped in the rigid classical tradition, was usually strict in his regard for the unity of time, but followed Shakespeare's example in freely violating that of place. His *Alchemist* has eleven scenes as against the eighteen of *Twelfth Night*, but *Catiline* has twenty as against the sixteen of *Julius Cæsar*. It is true that in confining his action, as in *The Alchemist*, to one house, Jonson persuaded himself that he was writing with greater propriety than Shakespeare, who like his own Puck was always ready to put a girdle round about the earth in forty minutes. Samuel Johnson, however, exposed this fallacy with his usual astuteness in writing of Nicholas Rowe's tragedies : " It is not less easy for the spectator to suppose himself at Athens in the second act, than at Thebes in the first." The truth is that Ben Jonson as a practising dramatist was as susceptible as Shakespeare to the conditions of his theatre ; but, unlike Shakespeare, he was partly in theoretical conflict with them. It should be added that his theory probably did little harm to his efficiency as a playwright on the Elizabethan stage. Unhappily we have little opportunity of judging this nowadays, but when I was myself producing *The Alchemist* I found his mastery of stagecraft hardly less complete than Shakespeare's own.

While, however, the difficulties of the proscenium stage in the matter of action are usually overcome in the more intelligent kind of Shakespearean production, those of intimate contact between the stage and the audience are not. Here the loss has been serious, and it is to be feared that it is not generally recognised as a loss at all. What the eye doesn't see the heart doesn't grieve is, I suppose, the sum of it, but to have visualised the life of a performance at The Globe, however dimly and imperfectly, is to realise what impoverishment in this respect is nearly always suffered by Shakespeare when he is acted in the theatres to-day.

The intimacy prevailed throughout the play. At every moment, the groundlings who had paid a penny to come in, and the richer sort who had paid from twopence to half-a-crown for the galleries, with something extra for a cushion or a seat, even sometimes a few favoured patrons accommodated on the stage itself, were all in as direct proximity with the players as the Sunday morning crowd with its orator on a tub in Hyde Park. Now and again – Ferdinand and Miranda in the cave is the commonly cited instance – an episode in the action would be withdrawn to a farther perspective, but with these rare exceptions the two hours' traffic of the stage was traffic in a particular sense. Even the quiet scenes, those between Rosalind and Orlando for example, had to be played right up to the eyes and ears of the audience. There was no effective frontier between the play and its public. Nothing like the convention of the fourth wall had been dreamt of, and the players neither could nor wished to pretend that they were not being overseen and overheard. In the proscenium-stage theatre it is considered, and rightly, to be abominable for an actor to play to the audience, though many actors and, if I may say so, more actresses, do it. On the Elizabethan stage the actor had to play to the audience or not at all, but the practice was robbed of offence, indeed it assumed positive merit, by the simple fact that the dramatists knew of this necessity, welcomed it, and used it in contriving most of their best effects.

Not to see this in the production of Shakespeare is, I repeat, to miss half the secret of his dramatic art. If the general movement of the play went forward in this intimacy, there were moments in almost every scene, and frequently whole scenes together, when the intimacy was heightened with what must have been startling and splendid results. Philip and John railing at each other before the walls of Angiers, Macbeth and Lady Macbeth wrestling in their conspiracy, Marc Antony mounted over Cæsar dead, Othello's

" by heaven he echoes me " as Iago debauches his understanding, Henry V crying " Once more unto the breach, dear friends," how breathlessly or with what mounting excitement must the Elizabethan motley have strained back to these imaginations bearing close upon them in the deep tides of great poetry or on the full blast of great rhetoric. To lose that throbbing interplay of emotion in performance is to lose who can say how much ?

Not only in these close-knit or heroic scenes of passion did the method score. The soliloquies also were intended by the poet to be spoken directly to the audience. The soliloquy has often in later days been censured as an unnatural device, and so it is when spoken with a ridiculous pretence that the player is talking aloud at length to himself or herself. The player under Shakespeare's direction talked to the audience, and then it was a very different matter. Hamlet murmuring " To be or not to be " in the distance like a minor introspect has but a slack hold on our attention, if he does not stray beyond it altogether, and when Viola in a coy pretence that there is nobody about enquires, " What means this lady ? " and goes on for twenty-five lines to consider how will this fadge, she becomes merely a tiresome girl who talks too much, and we wish she would go away so that we can get on wit! the next scene. But when Hamlet put all his quick-witted reasoning on suicide bluntly to the people about him, and Viola asked them point-blank what the devil she was going to do about it, they neither of them said a word too many for their own comfort or anybody's patience.

Research has placed the nature of the main structural features in Shakespeare's theatre beyond doubt. Minor aspects of Elizabethan stage operation will remain matters for dispute, but of certain things about the art that flourished on it we are sure. It was neither primitive nor crude ; it was highly civilised, expert, given hardly at all to experiment, but carrying an established tradition to its highest perfection. Shakespeare's originality did not consist in fugitive novelty. It was far profounder than that, and he looked for no frivolous aids from his stage. But he did look for a stage that could stand up even to his invention on level terms, and he found it.

CHAPTER VI

HIS ART

FROM time to time attempts are made to demonstrate that the theatre is a place for masks or marionettes, for expressionism or constructivism, for choral waves or something dimensional which I cannot recall. In these claims much sense is mixed with more nonsense. To their own scale I never hope to see anything lovelier than the marionettes of William Simmonds, and if a fine poet like W. B. Yeats and a fine decorator like Edmund Dulac conspire to make beauty in a drawing-room, that is so much profit to those who see it. Gordon Craig, who might have been one of the most notable men in the modern theatre, has chosen to be one of the most notable men out of it, but those who have stumbled along in it will forgive him for his woodcuts and the other enchanting things that he has done on paper. On the other hand, I have witnessed masqueradings, perpetrated on the stage in the name of advancement, that were but fooling, which I take to mean the activity of fools. The more exclusive German theatre of to-day is very partial to such entertainments.

Whatever the merits or follies of these enterprises may be, the art of Shakespeare had nothing

to do with any of them. They were, in the better
kind or the worse, not unknown to his age.
Gabriel Harvey and Philip Sidney were, not very
successfully, for classical metres in English, and
Lyly took the town with his *Euphues*. Shakespeare, the most sophisticated poet who ever
wrote, must have smiled as he contemplated these
smaller sophistries. In plain words, he had too
much to do to be bothered with them. They
belonged artistically to a world of unrest, and he
to a world of supreme composure. His purpose
was to tell tales that any lackey could understand, in terms of poetry that would storm Olym-
pus. He brought a superbly complicated art to
the achievement of a no less superbly simple
purpose. In this he was at one with most of the
great painters of the world, who have employed
their mastery in the production of what, in the
stupidest term that has ever infested the jargon
of art criticism, are called literary or anecdotal
pictures.

Everybody knows that Shakespeare is the
greatest English poet. Most people could not say
very clearly how they know it, but they could
with little difficulty of reference advance the
opinion of every critic of importance since his
time, from Jonson and Milton and Dryden
through Keats and Wordsworth and Arnold
down to Robert Bridges and Lascelles Aber-
crombie in support of their faith. We may take
it, in this case, that everybody is right. And yet

it is necessary in every new consideration of
Shakespeare to lay stress again on the fact that
he was a poet. Quite recently someone has been
seriously advocating that his language should be
modernised so that it may be readily intelligible
to a new age. This is silly, but it is significant.
For this cardinal point has to be realised about
Shakespeare before we can approach the truth
about him. His essential greatness lies not in his
plots or his humanity or his sense of character,
but in his poetry. Without this, the rest amount
to nothing beyond the reach of other men ; with
it, they become his and his alone.

Let us consider one of the simplest passages of
poetry in the plays, Brutus's :

> *O, that a man might know*
> *The end of this day's business ere it come.*
> *But it sufficeth that the day will end,*
> *And then the end is known.*

It might be said that this roughly means, " I
wish we knew what is going to happen ; but it
doesn't matter, we shall soon." But the whole
point is that it doesn't roughly mean that at all.
It doesn't even mean anything remotely resemb-
ling that. It means something quite different, and
what it means can be expressed only in one way :

> *O, that a man might know*
> *The end of this day's business ere it come.*
> *But it sufficeth that the day will end,*
> *And then the end is known.*

This is not that other meaning plus the adornment of great poetry, it is that other meaning transmuted by great poetry into something of a new kind. It is not the quality but the essential nature that has been changed. Indeed, it should not even be put like that. Shakespeare's lines are not a transmutation by great poetry of that other meaning, they are the expression of a different meaning conceived in terms of great poetry from the first.

This consideration has to be applied to the fabric of the plays as a whole. Their expression throughout, with negligible intervals, is that of great poetry, usually in verse but sometimes in prose. Again, it is not a case of simple tales adorned by great poetry. That is why any attempt to give a summary of the plays in other terms inevitably fails. You may discuss philosophic or technical questions raised by *Macbeth*, but you cannot say what *Macbeth* means nor what the story is except by repeating the play from the first word to the last. Moreover, the poetry of *Macbeth* is not only great poetry, it is great dramatic poetry. This does not mean that it is great poetry being used for the purposes of drama, but that it is great poetry which is drama. The tremendous moments in Shakespeare are not moments of sudden surprise in action, of unexpected discovery of character, of philosophic revelation, but of dramatic poetry. " Soft you, a word or two," " To-morrow and to-morrow and to-morrow," " Our revels now are ended," " O that a man might know," " I know when one is dead, and when one lives," " The rest is silence," " I am dying, Egypt, dying," " Thou art not conquered," " He's in Arthur's bosom," " This day is called the feast of Crispian," "What must the King do now ? " " I fluttered your Volscians in Corioli," " Ripeness is all," these things are not drama fortunate in the choice of perfect words ; they are perfect words, words moving in that utmost fullness of cadence, evocation, imagery, suggestion, when they become great poetry, kindled into great drama.

It was in his command of poetry as drama that Shakespeare's originality lay. Here he went beyond anything achieved before or since, and it is the sign of his supremacy. There is little that can be said about it. The magic cannot be explained, nor the significance paraphrased. But once we see it for what it is, and acknowledge its authority, our minds are free for the discussion of other and smaller aspects of Shakespeare's art. The fables of his plays were mostly not of his own invention, and his thought, though often profound, was also often taken ready-made from his age. Fable and thought alike were used by the dramatic poet, wrought into the texture of his poetry, and it made no odds to him whether they were original or borrowed. Once they had been reconceived in his creative moods, he no longer had to fear these inquisitions.

Shakespeare was the greatest English poet, and the greatest dramatic poet. But we need not go beyond that and claim that as an artist he never made mistakes. He did, and sometimes they were serious. We are not likely to detect them in his poetry, since his management of that is, with hardly a lapse, perfectly controlled. We search his works in vain for lines that are inadequate or inept. We must look rather at the material that he fused in his poetry. Here, too, we shall find that in general his control is unwavering, but now and again something seems to have gone wrong. We need take no notice of occasional slips, due perhaps to haste or even to corruptions of the text. And I have already explained that, in my opinion at least, such taxing of probability as we find in the conclusions of *The Two Gentlemen* and *Measure for Measure* should not be accounted as artistic errors at all, though in connection with these I may quote words of my own written elsewhere : " In both plays there is an apparently similar solution of difficulties in the last scene, made without any real reference to the characters as we have seen them in the play. And yet there is an essential difference. In *The Two Gentlemen of Verona* the reconciliation of the conflicting characters is made by Shakespeare with real conviction. He may not take very elaborate measures to persuade us that Valentine and Proteus could settle their differences in just this way, but he at least persuades us that he cares

Gs

very much that they should so settle them. Whatever failure there may be in the plot is due to the poet's lack of mastery. In *Measure for Measure*, on the other hand, the reconciliation, the redemption of Angelo, is made as a mere convenience to bring the play to an end. The play has been played out in a grasp of character that transcends event, and whatever failure of the plot there is now, is not due to the poet's lack of mastery, but to his indifference." This, I think, is true. Shakespeare was less concerned about the integrity of his plots when he was writing *Measure for Measure* than when he wrote *The Two Gentlemen*, but in both plays, nevertheless, he made an arbitrary ending because he had no ready means of making a logical one. And in either case we should not be troubled by something of relative unimportance. The grace and charm of the one play, the dark splendour of the other, would gain nothing by a tidier end. The faults of which I speak are of a more fundamental kind. I cannot attempt to make a catalogue of these, but will consider two examples, to be found in the presentation of the characters of Lear and Shylock.

Lear is by common consent one of the supreme masterpieces of tragic drama. In some respects we may give the palm to *Hamlet* or *Othello* or *Macbeth*, but all things considered *Lear* is Shakespeare's highest performance in tragedy. It, above the rest – and how high is that – has a sublimity that is not outdone by Aeschylus

himself. Nevertheless, *Lear* has one defect that
always teases my admiration. Why, at the
beginning of the play, does Lear behave towards
Cordelia like a cross-grained and unreasonable
old fool ? He has told the court of his intention
to retire from active kingship in order to enjoy
the quieter blessings of old age, but not a word
had been said indicating that his mind is giving
way or that there is anything in the state of his
affairs threatening to unhinge it. On the contrary, he is clearly, from his opening words, in
full possession of his reason. And then, suddenly,
he breaks out upon Cordelia, the child who has
been " our joy, although our last not least," in
an insensate rage that her perfectly dutiful and
loving answer has done nothing whatever to
provoke. Kent boldly tells him he is mad, and
gets banished for his pains. And I for one, when
I read or see the play, am left longing to call out
to Lear that he is conducting himself outrageously,
and that if trouble is coming to him he has very
wilfully asked for it.

The difficulty here is not at all the same as that
at the end of *Measure for Measure*. There, character is forced to the poet's convenience, but it is
after its development through the play. We know
by now just what Angelo is, and his sudden
conversion may in itself appear incredible, but
it does not at all loosen the foundations on which
his character has been built. We merely say
that it is unlikely that such a man would behave

so, and leave it at that. But in Lear this violation of probability comes before we know anything about him. We are asked to believe that an old man who has just appeared before us for the first time, a much honoured King and clear in his wits, would without warning treat his beloved daughter with entirely gratuitous cruelty, and while he is yet protesting that he " loved her most " call her every name short of bitch he can lay his tongue to. It is on this foundation that we are now to see the tragedy of Lear's life and character unfold, and I can never get away from the feeling that there is something radically unsound about it. Within a few scenes Shakespeare's spell, working at the very height of its potency, will be on us again, and slowly the memory of our misgivings will fade. But it is a bad start; in itself, I think, indefensible. Shakespeare's recovery is such that anything can be excused, but here surely excuse is necessary. The defiance of probability, an acceptable convention at the end of *Measure for Measure*, is a grave misjudgement at the opening of *Lear*.

The mistake in *Lear*, bad as it is, is isolated at the beginning of the play, and Shakespeare, with an imaginative power that he himself hardly equals elsewhere, managed to escape its consequences. The case of Shylock is a good deal more complicated. Ever since Shakespeare created him his character has been under discussion. For a time he held the stage as a comic

figure, a sport for baiting. Henry Irving, at the
other extreme, invested him with tragic pity,
sending him to defeat before a sympathetic
audience. Neither view, I think, is altogether
right or altogether wrong. *The Merchant of
Venice*, clearly, was designed as a comedy, and
Shakespeare at first can have had no intention of
allowing a comic villain to turn tragic hero on his
hands. And yet, to some extent, that is what
happened, as it happened in a modified sense with
Malvolio. Step by step Shakespeare found
Shylock becoming not the butt of a comic mood
but the victim of circumstance, and the tragic
note began to assert itself would he or not.
At the time – 1595 or so – the poet had created
Richard II and Romeo, but none of his vaster
tragic figures, and through Shylock intimations
of a latent power began to stir in him. As the
Jew took shape, he made more claims for himself
than could be dismissed quite to the convenience
of comedy. And so, between the first conception
and the created whole, a change, I think, took
place in Shakespeare's attitude towards his
invention.

There was nothing amiss with this in itself. It
was the sort of thing that might upset Ben Jonson,
but Shakespeare was quite capable of proving
wiser than the rules that he broke. The development of character, even though it be from one
key to another, has long since been accepted as a
legitimate dramatic effect ; indeed, it is generally

regarded as a merit. Also, in Shakespeare's own time, the merging of tragedy with comedy was an established practice, offensive as it might be to the purists. In principle there is nothing the matter with the character of Shylock. But in effect Shakespeare's divided or inconstant purpose has led him, as it seems to me, into a pitfall at a crucial moment.

Shakespeare obviously meant the trial scene to be the great event of his play, as it is. Shylock, with an unappeasable ferocity that almost becomes heroic, insists on the penalty nominated in his bond. No pleas of interest or mercy can turn him for a moment from his purpose of executing legal murder of the most atrocious kind on Antonio. Whatever spark of sympathy may have been lit in us during the earlier scenes by his domestic calamities and his tribal passion, is quenched as we watch this pitiless persecution. The man is revealed as the inexorable dog that Gratiano calls him, and we too heartily hope that he may be damned. Then, with Portia's sentence, the blow falls, and we are satisfied. Shylock is satisfactorily damned – but what is Shakespeare to do with him now? That is where he tripped. To send Shylock off in derision, which is what he deserves, would be to overlook those tragic aspects of his character that have been glancing through the comedy, and would go against the grain. And so this is what happens. Shylock consents to take thrice the sum forfeited, an offer already made. No, says Portia, it must now be the pound of flesh or nothing. Shylock asks if he can have his principal. No. Not barely his principal? No. Then he must go, and the devil give them good for it. But he may not even go. He has conspired mortally against a citizen, and his goods and life are at the discretion of the court. A composition is made which leaves Shylock a broken man, and under pledge, very objectionably imposed by Antonio, to become a Christian. And so Shakespeare, almost in desperation it seems, piles up the agony against him at the last moment so that he may go out of the court stripped of everything else, it may be, but not of every vestige of his tragic dignity. But it simply will not do. When Shylock says :

> *Nay, take my life and all ; pardon not that :*
> *You take my house when you do take the prop*
> *That doth sustain my house : you take my life*
> *When you do take the means whereby I live —*

unless we are bluffed by a sentimental piece of acting, we are sickened. This alleged cry from the depths of a suffering soul becomes, if we have in mind the action as a whole, the whine of an inhuman ruffian who has been kicked. Thus at the climax of a play that none but he could have written, Shakespeare, I think, makes another serious error of judgement. I may note that Mr. Dover Wilson comes to an entirely opposite conclusion. Shakespeare, he says, " shows us everything of Shylock's meanness, cunning and cruelty . . . and notwithstanding he compels the best of us, and the best in us, to cry out with Heine's ' Fair Briton ' upon the Jew's exit, ' By heaven, the man is wronged ! ' " All I can say is that he makes the best in me cry out nothing of the sort.

No poet, however, in all the list of them could so gloriously afford to make lapses, even grave lapses, from perfection. When to-day we examine his plays, however untutored we may be, we examine them not as they came from his pen, but as they come to us tried and tried again in the critical fires of three hundred years. They are too lovely, too admirable, to be accepted on hearsay, and so we study them for ourselves with what freshness of mind we may. And always we find ourselves confirming the judgement of the ages. Here is a body of work that not only in creative power but in sustained excellence of workmanship is the best that has been done by a race rightly proud of its theatre and its poetry. It is pleasant, in a world of conflicting ideas, to have one thing at least about which everybody is agreed.

CHAPTER VII

HIS MIND

PHILOSOPHY, says the dictionary, is " the science of being as being : the knowledge of the causes and laws of all phenomena." I take this to mean that philosophy is concerned with the deduction of abstract principles from particular instances. I will confess that my attempts to read the philosophers have not been very rewarding, chiefly because most of the time I could not understand what they were saying. Fortunately for my present needs I have no occasion to venture out of my depth. I know, at least, what philosophy primarily proposes to itself to do, and I know that it is not what poetry primarily proposes to itself to do. Since the mind of man is not a machine but a flexible organism, every mind will, I suppose, be a bit of everything, and the philosopher and the poet each will stray, by accident or design, now and again into the other's territory. But in the main the distinction is clear enough.

The purpose of poetry is to see as intensely as possible those particular instances from which philosophy formulates its principles, and to give them the most striking form which it can devise. It is concerned not so much with the causes and laws of all phenomena as with the phenomena

themselves. It is the poet's faith that to see a
thing vividly is to understand it – that in the
image of the thing itself are revealed the causes
and laws that govern its nature. The representation of the thing seen is the function of his art,
and an infinitely complicated business it is. So
complicated that it is a common device of the
poet to represent the thing seen by placing some
other thing before us.

I am aware that poetry constantly appears to
be going beyond, or wide of, this commission. It
speculates, it dogmatises, it aspires, it complains.
Nevertheless, the governing condition of its being,
to which it always has to return in submission, is
this perception and representation of phenomena ;
not, it need hardly be added, only material
phenomena, since falling in love, for example,
may be the thing perceived and represented.

The measure of a poet's mind then is not its
aptness for philosophical abstraction, but its capacity for receiving vivid impressions of a great
variety of phenomena, impressions upon which
his art will work in the creation of his poetry. In
this capacity Shakespeare's mind was probably the
most richly endowed that the world has known.

Nothing escaped that burning gaze, that intent
contemplation. The features of every phenomenon that he encountered were registered in his
mind with matchless fidelity. Habits, character,
countenances, costume, landscape, emotions, sea-
sonal changes, state affairs, events witnessed,

reports heard and chronicles read, traffic in the
streets and stars in the heavens, misery and pomp
and vice and honour, health and sickness, vigour,
frailty, stenches and sweet smells, cunning and
pity, birds and animals and games – every shape
and condition and element of his eager daily
experience became a fixed and glowing image in
his mind for use as his art should require. There
they underwent infinite scrutiny and permuta-
tions, one illuminating another, the material
of life shaping slowly, yet with an untold fertility, towards the strictly organised purposes of
art. Shakespeare in this did as other poets do,
but he excelled them all at once in the lavishness
and the precision with which the images were
recorded.

This abnormally acute power of perception
meant a correspondingly acute sensibility of mood.
Earlier in this book I have spoken of the happiness
that he must have enjoyed during the years of his
crowded creation. But it was not a happiness that
precluded seasons of deep and melancholy gloom,
and there is ample evidence in his work that he
knew all that mortal stress could be. It is not
a case of seeing in the spiritual strife of *Hamlet* or
Lear a direct reflection of his own spirit in travail.
It is quite possible for either of these plays to have
been written during a time of unclouded personal
peace. But through and through the sonnets and
the plays, tragedies and comedies alike, are woven
dark threads of suffering for which no impersonal

theory can wholly account. The known continuity and abundance of his work between the ages of twenty-seven and forty-seven is sufficient proof that for twenty years at least his prime was remarkable in vigour, and there is certainly nothing to show that he was at any time an ailing man. I think it is a mistake to regard even Aubrey's scrap of evidence, " he was in pain," as suggesting more than slight and rather convenient indisposition. But whatever the pathological truth may be there can be no doubt that Shakespeare, in the long glory of his invention, suffered many dejected, even despairing moods.

With speculative thought Shakespeare's mind was not greatly concerned. His views on social, theological, political, scientific and such themes are mostly those current in his time, and if he takes a side it is not commonly that of a minority. He was even ready to accept popular superstitions and, whether he believed in them or not, to make use of them in his plays. It may amuse us to decide on the evidence of *Coriolanus* that Shakespeare hated mobs, but this kind of thing is but matter for a May morning. The only subject on which Shakespeare steadily explores, or rather demonstrates, the profounder issues of philosophy is that of tragic retribution. The expiation of offence in disaster is a theme that he treats consistently with intellectual passion. It is, I think, the only one of which this can be said. He constantly introduces into his plays passages of shrewd and moving worldly wisdom, memorably expressed, but these are no more than marginal notes to philosophy. His world is one of consummately realised images, and richer in the ranging of phenomena than any that we know. Shakespeare enters no claim to be reckoned among the philosophers, but a philosopher with nothing but Shakespeare's plays to work upon might construct a system that would not discredit his mystery.

Something must be said of the environment in which Shakespeare worked. The society of his own theatrical and literary fellowship was a bracing one, and the conditions of his calling, as I have already said, were favourable. He moved among the best wit and gaiety and learning of his time, and although he was probably not a very spectacular person, we may be sure that his society was sought by men worthy to enjoy it. But Elizabethan squalor was as striking as Elizabethan splendour, and Shakespeare must have been as sensible of the one as the other. Filth flowed in the streets ; horrible scenes were of frequent occurrence at public executions ; licensed but ill-managed brothels were places of contagion and death ; the highways, even the city thoroughfares were infested by footpads and cut-throats ; vermin swarmed in the house-timbers ; brutal sports were the entertainment of fashion. On a clear summer afternoon at the end of Elizabeth's reign a spectator on the north side of the river,

situated we will imagine on the tower-top of old
St. Paul's, would have looked across the Thames,
Thamesis Fluvius of the cartographers, to Southwark. And there on Bankside he would see the
theatres, The Swan and The Globe, with their
flags up if performances were on. He would see
Winchester House, the London episcopal seat of
that diocese. But near at hand he would also see
the bull and bear baiting rings, and the public
stews known as Holland's Leaguer, under an early
print of which is inscribed these verses :

> *Unto this Island and great Pluto's Court,*
> *None are deny'd that willingly resort,*
> *Charon o'er Phlegeton will set on shoare,*
> *And Cerberus will guard you to the door*
> *Where dainty Devils, drest in human shape,*
> *Upon your senses soon will make a rape.*
> *They that come freely to this house of sinne*
> *In Hell as freely may have entrance in.*

The little boat-sails on the water looked clean
enough, but beyond them lay much festering
impurity. Morals apart, and morals are mislead-
ing anyway, the dirt was dreadful. What policing
there was lived on corruption rather than wages.
Foul infections walked the byways. Altogether
it was, to our modern imagination, a discouraging
scene. It seems to us that the entire population
ought to have died out in a year. But it did not :
it thrived. And in the midst of it thrived also
Shakespeare and his theatre, dramatising great

poetry for an eager robust public and a magnificent court. It all seems very odd. And yet, perhaps not so odd after all.

For are we any better to-day? Certainly we are cleaner : there is great gain in that. But if we read the daily records of any popular newspaper, do we find that we are less brutal, less obscene, less corrupt? It is hateful to think it, but I fear that if there were to be a public execution in Trafalgar Square to-morrow the thoroughfares would be blocked from Piccadilly to St. Martin's Lane. Some speed-maniac fails to break a record and perhaps kills himself, and he covers the front pages : Sir Ronald Ross, one of the loveliest spirits of the modern world and one of the greatest benefactors to mankind, dies, and the event claims an obscure paragraph. A dope-sodden wench drives an unfortunate magistrate to his wit's end, and the world is asked to hold its breath ; the milk-supply on which a million infant lives depend is saved, and for all the notice that is taken it might have been saved in the middle of the Sahara desert. Shakespeare in the amenities of his mind had much to contend with ; but he would have found many provocations to-day.

" Tennyson, although he was vitally interested in life, and honest enough in his acceptance of the processes of life so far as he could interpret them, had also certain abstract moral points of view which he was apt to impose upon those processes in course of creation . . . it is one of the chief glories of Shakespeare's art that it is intensely concerned with life, with its moral consequences, but hardly at all concerned with moral points of view that are not directly the consequence of life as it grows at the poet's bidding. That is why we feel that Shakespeare loved Macbeth, whose moral conduct he must have condemned, no less than Rosalind, whose conduct he as certainly sanctioned." I wrote these words ten years ago, in a study of Victorian poetry, and they express an idea that has always been steadily at the centre of my thought about Shakespeare. His delight, his passion, was to understand the world, not to pass judgement on it. In the understanding, judgement might be an implication from which there was no escape, as in the dramas of expiation. Othello, Macbeth, Brutus, these men are victimised by demons that can be exorcised only by destruction. The tragedy in each case is not that the sin has to draw the wage of death, but that with the sin dies also a man of much nobility. Even Macbeth, whose crime is the most inexcusable, was a poet fatally flawed by the weakness that was exploited by his wife's iron will. There is no place in Shakespeare's cosmology for the doctrine of reclamation. When great evil has been done, it cannot be redeemed on earth by penitence. Such transgressors can only find the light, if light there be, by passing through that darkness from which no traveller returns. It is a terrible belief, but it was an article of Shakespeare's poetic faith, and it has a grandeur which has been sanctioned by most of the great tragic poets of the world. When Shakespeare discarded it, as he did in the case of Angelo, his heart was not in a solution that was impos:ble to the great tragedies. Here the protagonists had to pay the penalty. He could not spare these men, but neither could he bear them any malice. The nobility was overthrown in the catastrophe that the offence demanded, but it remained a nobility to lament in noble terms. "For he was great of heart," says Cassio as Othello lies dead before him. For Macbeth dead there is no word of pity from enemies for whom he is the bloodier villain than terms can give him out ; he expected none. But as the end approaches Shakespeare sets him speaking for himself of the happier way that he knows ambition should have trod :

> *I have liv'd long enough : my way of life*
> *Is fall'n into the sear, the yellow leaf ;*
> *And that which should accompany old age,*
> *As honour, love, obedience, troops of friends,*
> *I must not look to have . . .*

The pity is there ; not from his enemies, but it is not self-pity. It is the pity of his maker, showing him for a moment erect in moral disaster, a man who might have worthily enjoyed these most worthy things. And for Brutus dead, claimed by a necessity no less inexorable than that of Macbeth himself, what words are found :

Hs

This was the noblest Roman of them all. . . .
His life was gentle ; and the elements
So mix'd in him, that Nature might stand up,
And say to all the world, " This was a man ! "

" His life was gentle " : this from Antony of the
man who loved Cæsar well, and slew him. The
mercy of reprieve in these larger tragic issues it
was beyond Shakespeare's power to bestow, but,
atonement made, there was in the chronicle of
these poor lives an infinity of mercy to season
justice.

If I could ask Shakespeare one question about
his life, I think it would be, " Why did you retire
to Stratford in 1611, and what did you do afterwards ? " Apart from the fact that I suspect that
I should learn of lost masterpieces, lyric or otherwise, the question may, perhaps, be set down to no
better than idle curiosity, since the answer might
not throw any fresh light on the real Shakespeare
whom we know, the Essential Shakespeare, as
Mr. Dover Wilson calls him. And yet it might.

The problem, for it is that, has been warmly
debated. Some authorities think that Shakespeare having made his modest pile at the age of
forty-seven, felt that he had borne the brunt of
theatrical enterprise long enough, and decided
for a quiet life in the little midland town where he
had so many agreeable ties. There is nothing
inherently unreasonable in this view, which might
very well turn out to be the correct one. Others,

again, have seen in the retirement the flight of a
sick man from scenes where he had suffered almost
to the loss of reason. These are the critics who lay
strong emphasis on the personal interpretation of
the plays. They see in the stress of the great
tragedies, and particularly of *Lear* (1607), a clear
indication that the poet himself was passing
through a period of dark spiritual strife. In
Antony, Coriolanus, Cymbeline and *The Winter's Tale*,
they discern a gradual recovery of balance, which
is finally restored in the last purgation of *The
Tempest* in 1611, after which he knew that the
virtue had gone out of him, and departed. An
attempt is sometimes made to present this view
more credibly by transferring *Timon of Athens* from
1608, its usually accepted date, to 1609 or 1610.
I do not personally think it matters when *Timon*
was written. It is certainly a play full of very
strange madness, but even if substantially it is
Shakespeare's work at all, I never read anything
that seemed to me to have less of the stamp of
autobiography upon it. In any case, this personal-
interpretation method is full of snares. Any
knowledge of creative processes tells us that a poet
can depict great agony without having endured it
himself.

At the same time, there is something attractive,
and more than a little plausible, in the conception
of *The Tempest* as denoting the reconciliation of
Shakespeare's mind with life after being at odds,
" port after stormy seas." There is, no doubt,

something in this. But the attractiveness should
not tempt us to conjectures that will make it more
attractive still. *The Tempest*, so far as we know,
was the last play that Shakespeare wrote ; but I
confess that, whenever I read or see it, the notion
of regarding the lovely closing scenes as a drama-
tisation of the poet's farewell to the stage always
strikes me as ludicrous. Really, Shakespeares do
not work like that.

In another place I wrote : " If we do not attach
too much importance to our fancy, we may very
well see in the development, over twenty years of
crowded working-life, from the light-hearted deft-
ness of *Love's Labour's Lost* and *The Two Gentlemen
of Verona*, the dewy poetry of *A Midsummer Night's
Dream*, the lusty theatrical vigour and mastery
of the histories, through the humanity of the
maturer comedies, and then the profound moral
passion of the tragedies, to the peace and intellectual certainty of *The Tempest*, a chart of
Shakespeare's spiritual life." Beyond that it is
unwise to go. But the problem of the retirement
in 1611 remains. Whatever may have happened
to Shakespeare's mind in the creation of *Lear* or
even of *Timon*, there is abundant evidence that in
The Tempest it had recovered serene possession of
itself. There is not a trace of weariness or failing
power in the play. If malady of the mind there
had been, it had passed, and although the reconciliation theory may be accepted with discretion,
I find no suggestion anywhere that the poet was

consciously engaged in his closing task. On the
contrary, in the manifest joy of the writing I see
the best possible reason for believing that here
was a poet with an immense capacity for work
still to come. No sign has been discovered of
what then happened, beyond the bare fact that
between 1611 and his death Shakespeare did, part
of the time at any rate, live at Stratford. When he
retired his invention was not exhausted ; splen-
didly far from it. How then did he use it there-
after ? That he deliberately put down his pen and
left The Globe for unemployment in a small town,
seems unlikely in the extreme. If he could answer
the question of my choice, should we perhaps learn
that he was writing during those last years, not
for the theatre, but in fulfilment of a design that
had decided him to leave London for the seclusion
of New Place ? This is my one indulgence in
guess-work concerning Shakespeare : it is, I
cannot but think, somewhere near the mark. At
least it offers a rational explanation of what otherwise I find inexplicable.

CHAPTER VIII

EPILOGUE

In this brief attempt to examine something of Shakespeare's mind and art in relation to his life and the conditions in which he worked, I have kept one consideration always at hand as I wrote. Shakespeare was a practical playwright, intent, and very successfully intent, on providing entertainment for an audience in the theatre. He was other things as well ; perhaps greater things. He was a poet, illuminating the human spirit and the springs of human conduct with a clarity and magic that have never been excelled, have, on the whole, never been equalled. But the most immediate aspect of his plays, and the one that must always chiefly take the attention of mankind, is that of men and women in swift, turbulent, racy action that gives us the impression of life as we know it on the surface of daily experience, and does its profounder business reticently, by implication, in deep undertones that remain with us in revelation long after the heat and resonance of the scene have passed away.

In other words, Shakespeare, while he was investigating character with his matchless poetic acumen, was also peopling his stage for the world's delight with an astonishing variety of characters. Professor Saintsbury, a critic who has made a lifelong habit of being right about most things, wrote thirty-five years ago : " With that supreme genius that distinguishes him from the common playwright, Shakespeare has never made his heroes or heroines types ; and this has puzzled many, and driven not a few to despairing efforts to make them out types after all." It is the great good luck of the English drama and the English theatre that the playwright who most repays critical enquiry is also the playwright who generation after generation has most successfully held the stage against all comers.

Shelley, in saying that poets are the unacknowledged legislators of the world, could have said it of no one so truly as of Shakespeare. Shakespeare's influence on the English mind, and so on the English character, is far beyond calculation. Millions of his countrymen in the course of time have delightedly watched the pageant of his plays, to be influenced and enlightened quite above their reckoning. An intimacy with this poet's theatre is in itself a liberal enfranchisement of the mind. Well might the young Keats exclaim, " I am very near agreeing with Hazlitt that Shakespeare is enough for us."

The age that succeeded Shakespeare was alive to his greatness, but thought him loose in construction, coarse in diction, undisciplined in art. Dryden, the greatest critic of his time and the most generous towards Shakespeare, led the way in expressions of this kind. We have recovered from these delusions, and they are not likely to be current again. It is possible that if we could talk with Shakespeare we should have difficulty in understanding his speech ; we cannot tell how rapidly the sound of language changes, though modern mechanism will inform our children if they are curious to know. But Shakespeare's word, as we have it through the blessed foresight of John Heminge and Henry Condell, remains after three centuries the subtlest, the most eloquent, the loveliest that we know. And as for his form, careful examination of it on the stage reveals that also as being at the top of English achievement.

> *Not marble, nor the gilded monuments*
> *Of princes, shall outlive this powerful rhyme.*

It was a proud boast, deliberate in its high-pitched arrogance. And yet it was the simple statement of a simple truth. Where there is no vision, the people perish. It is consoling, in a world of many betrayals and dishonours, to reflect that this visionary excellence really does outlast all. This poet died knowing how imperfect was his knowledge, but his understanding was to be the glory of our heritage.

NOTE ON BOOKS

THERE are several cheap editions of Shakespeare's Works in handy form. *The Arden Shakespeare* (Methuen), a play to a volume, edited by recognised authorities with ample notes and introductions, may be recommended to readers who want something more elaborate at a small cost.

A Life of William Shakespeare, by Sidney Lee (Smith Elder), is the standard biography.

William Shakespeare. A Study of Facts and Problems, by E. K. Chambers, 2 vols. (Oxford) is a masterly survey of the whole field of Shakespearean scholarship and criticism.

The Shakespeare-Allusion Book, 2 vols. (Oxford), contains all known direct and indirect allusions to Shakespeare between the years 1591–1700.

Dr. Pierce Butler's *Materials for the Life of Shakespeare*, (Oxford), is a compact *précis* of the primary sources of information about Shakespeare's life.

Studies in the First Folio (Oxford), contains an authoritative examination by various scholars of the aspects and problems presented by the corner-stone of all Shakespearean literature.

Mr. Leslie Hotson's *Shakespeare versus Shallow* (Nonesuch Press) is an admirable example of the intensive research that distinguishes one branch of Shakespearean learning. Mr. Percy Allen's *The Oxford-Shakespeare Case Corroborated* (Palmer), is representative of its school.

Shakespeare Criticism. Edited by D. Nichol Smith (World's Classics) is a useful selection, which ' attempts to give the greatest pieces of Shakespeare criticism from 1623 to 1840.'

Among the many books that in recent years have been a credit to Shakespearean criticism, special note may be made of Mr. Harley Granville-Barker's *Prefaces*, 2 vols. (Sidgwick & Jackson), which are important essays in elucidation tested by stage practice.